GREAT PEOPLE IN HISTORY

GREAT ARTISTS

GREAT PEOPLE IN HISTORY

GREAT ARTISTS

Charlotte Gerlings

ROSEN
PUBLISHING®

New York

This edition published in 2013 by:

The Rosen Publishing Group, Inc.
29 East 21st Street, New York, NY 10010

Cover images (left ot right): Detail from The Garden of
Earthly Delights by Hieronymus Bosch; Mona Lisa by
Leonardo da Vinci; detail from The Chair and the Pipe
by Vincent van Gogh

Library of Congress Cataloging-in-Publication Data

Gerlings, Charlotte.
  Great artists / Charlotte Gerlings.
      pages cm. -- (Great people in history)
  Includes bibliographical references and index.
  ISBN 978-1-4777-0401-1 (library binding)
  1. Artists--Juvenile literature. I. Title.
  N42.G47 2013
  700.92'2--dc23
  [B]
                                        2012032159

Manufactured in China

SL002552US

CPSIA Compliance Information: Batch W13YA: For
further information, contact Rosen Publishing, New
York, New York, at 1-800-237-9932

Contents

Introduction

It is a pleasant but far from simple task to pick "great" artists from the hundreds of possibilities. Everyone has a range of favorites, and a geographical spread is necessary too. With the early settlers, the European art tradition crossed the Atlantic to the New World, and traveled with traders to the Far East. This book helps to show how that tradition was reinterpreted in different locations. Inevitably, my editors and I had to make many reluctant omissions, and the constraints of copyright affected the choice of twentieth-century and contemporary artists. However, the selection that follows is intended to take readers on a wide-ranging journey through the story of western art, with the aid of examples of its leading exponents. For the most part, they have trained, inspired, or influenced one another from the thirteenth century to the present day. It is a fascinating, ever-developing part of our lives that we shall never tire of looking at.

Major exhibitions are a feature of galleries in every principal city nowadays. Curators put years of planning and negotiation into assembling "blockbuster" shows of both old and modern masters, whose works are borrowed and transported all over the world. Yet we must remember that we can go to the same galleries at other times, simply to view their standing exhibitions; and the youngest of gallery visitors are often given a special welcome. National and provincial galleries not only house famous works but also give us the opportunity to discover the paintings of less well-known artists. These people frequently worked alongside the great names, sharing ideas and techniques, sometimes in the role of teacher or pupil.

Standing in front of a Renaissance picture by the likes of Botticelli or Titian, for example, it is hard to imagine that the painters and sculptors we admire were originally classified as "mere" craftsmen. Most came from humble backgrounds and were accepted into a studio around the age of nine. At first, they earned their keep by cleaning and running errands, gradually working up from apprentice to journeyman and finally master. The fresco painter Cennini has left this daunting account of the Renaissance apprentice's training schedule: "Start first of all by grinding colors, boiling up glue, mixing plaster, then going on to prepare panels, retouching them,

Detail from **The Mystic Nativity** *(1500) by Sandro Botticelli*

polishing them, applying gold leaf, learning how to grain. Then another six years to study the use of color, the application of mordants, to find out how to paint draperies and folds and how to work in fresco. And all the time you must practice drawing…work-day and feast-day."

If an artist graduated to set up his own studio, the process began all over again with swarms of apprentices surrounded by the tools and materials of the business, in pursuit of lucrative commissions. The masters who became Court painters had rather more security—as long as they pleased their patrons—but their status was often that of a servant or palace workman. Some fresco painters, for example, were paid only by the amount of wall they covered. Occasionally, an astute artist like Rubens was elevated to the rank of diplomat.

Detail taken from **Marie de Medici Disembarking at Marseilles After Marriage to Henry IV of France** *by Peter Paul Rubens (1622–25)*

The more we examine the great artists of all periods, the more we appreciate that, no matter how sublime their work, they were touched by the events of history as much as the next person. Their lives were disrupted by wars, transformed by scientific discoveries, cut short by the medieval plague or twentieth-century influenza.

To treat our subjects as fully as possible, each one occupies their own double-page spread containing two pictures, a commentary, and a timeline that points to the principal events of his or her life. The selection of some less familiar pictures will, I hope, broaden appreciation and encourage a fresh approach. Occasionally, I have combined a pair, where the connection is particularly interesting or useful. Where the commentary mentions an artist with his or her own entry in the book, that name appears in **bold type** for easy reference. For the same reason, the arrangement is alphabetical, incidentally making for some remarkable neighbors.

It is hoped that this book may be enjoyed as a reference by students and practicing artists, and a companion to the general reader who loves looking at pictures and is interested in finding out how skills and personal style come through in service of the creative process.

Charlotte Gerlings

Fra Angelico

Timeline

1387(?)	Born Guido di Pietro in Vicchio di Mugello, Tuscany, Italy
1407	Enters Dominican monastery at Fiesole, near Florence
1409–14	Papal politics exile monks to Foligno, in Umbria
1414–18	Plague drives them to Cortona
1419–35	Returns long-term to Fiesole, becomes Fra Giovanni
1433	Commissioned to paint the Linenworkers' Triptych
1436–45	Commissioned by Cosimo de' Medici, decorates Convent of San Marco, Florence
1445	Invited to Rome by Pope Eugenius IV. Paints portrait of Charles VII of France
1447	Begins frescoes in Capella di San Brizio, Orvieto
1447–49	Travels to Rome with pupil Gozzoli to paint frescoes of SS Stephen and Lawrence in Vatican's Capella Niccolina
1449–52	Returns to Fiesole, elected Prior
1455	Returns to Rome, where he dies

Fra Angelico and his brother Benedetto both joined the Dominican Order of Preachers in 1407. At their monastery in Fiesole, the young men were directed to illuminating manuscripts, and it is possible they remained in artistic partnership for most of their lives.

Fra Angelico soon gained a reputation for his technical skills in composition and color and was promoted to overseeing a busy workshop inside the Order. His religious title was Fra Giovanni but the other friars nicknamed him "Angelico" for his piety and the beautiful work that he produced. He is reputed never to have altered or retouched any of his paintings, firmly believing that to do so would have been against God's will.

Nothing is known of Fra Angelico's early teachers, other than the influence he shows of the Sienese school. Angelico and Benedetto probably made the leap to full-scale fresco painting during the five years that their order was exiled in the Umbrian hill town of

Deposition of Christ *(detail) (1436–45)*

The frescoes in the convent of San Marco decorated both the communal spaces and the nuns' private cells, where they were designed to encourage meditation. Fra Angelico's experience as an illuminator shows in his thin, precise application of paint. It was an ideal method for detailing wing feathers and embroidery, and well suited to background features, as shown in this detail.

Foligno. **Giotto**'s frescoes at Assisi would have been within easy reach and the brothers are certain to have visited them.

Once he had moved to Florence at the invitation of Cosimo de' Medici and started decorating the convent of San Marco, Fra Angelico's handling of form, perspective, and color developed even further. Benedetto is said to have worked alongside his brother on the vast San Marco commission, and one of their apprentices was the young Benozzo Gozzoli.

The Altarpiece of San Marco *(1436–45)*

Fra Angelico had an innovative approach to composition and he is credited with the invention of the sacra conversazione, *a device that places all the figures in a painting close to one another, as though in conversation. Although the Renaissance meant a strong move toward humanism, Fra Angelico's work maintained a firm reverence for the Christian ideal.*

Giuseppe Arcimboldo

Timeline

Vertumnus *(detail) (1591)*

A magnificent portrait of Rudolf II as the ancient Roman god of vegetation and the changing seasons. Vertumnus was also the symbol of commerce. The emperor was delighted with the idea of himself as the embodiment of fruitfulness, harmony, and a strong economy, and awarded Arcimboldo the title of Count Palatine.

Giuseppe Arcimboldo was an artist of great ingenuity. Pre-dating the Surrealists by over three hundred years, his compositions of painted flowers, vegetables, and other more bizarre objects took the sixteenth-century Hapsburg Court by storm. Three successive emperors, Ferdinand I, Maximilian II, and Rudolf II, became devotees of his extraordinary portrait series.

In 1562, Arcimboldo answered an imperial invitation and left Milan for Prague. There he assumed the post of Court painter and decorator, events organizer, costume designer, and all-round art adviser. Along with royal weddings, festivities at Court consisted of pageants and tournaments. The Uffizi in Florence has a red leather folder, dedicated to Rudolf II. Inside are 148 of Arcimboldo's pen and wash sketches detailing costumes and "props" for various events based on classical allegory. These extravaganzas were designed to display the Hapsburgs' dynastic power to hundreds of high-ranking guests.

The Uffizi portfolio is a very rare item, as little of Arcimboldo's signed work survives; nor did he leave any writings, although he is known to have been highly educated. His talents spanned the arts, sciences, engineering, and philosophy; he was a true "Renaissance man." Yet for no obvious reason, his work sank into obscurity until rediscovered in the nineteenth century.

Water *from* "The Four Elements" *(1566)*
As a young man, Arcimboldo painted stained glass for Milan
Cathedral, but it was through tapestry design that his richly ornamental
style emerged, to mature in the painted series of "Seasons" and
"Elements." Arcimboldo was to copy Water *many times, for gifts to*
impress their recipients with the glory of the Hapsburgs.

Giovanni Bellini

Timeline

Giovanni Bellini is responsible for raising the standard of the Venetian school of painting to the point where the city rivaled Florence as a center of Renaissance excellence. His father, brother, and brother-in-law were artists too, but it is the latter, Andrea Mantegna (1431–1503), who initially spurred Bellini on to painting landscapes and defining the mood of a picture.

Like all his Italian contemporaries, Bellini was used to working in water-based tempera on wooden panels or plaster walls. However, once he had seen the work of Rogier van der Weyden (*c.*1400–1464), he was eager to try the Flemish oil glazing technique brought to Venice by Antonello da Messina in 1475.

Bellini was always experimenting with his art. Now, with the rich translucence of oil glazes at his fingertips—revealing new depths to familiar colors and demanding a different type of brushwork—he uncovered a wealth of possibilities. When Bellini learned how to translate the Venetian play of light between sky and water, he had the key to all the subtle harmonies and brilliant colors that would come to signify the school of Venice for the next two centuries.

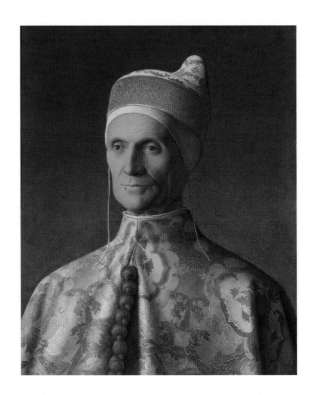

Doge Leonardo Loredan *(c.1501)*

The ruler of Venice wears gold damask robes, an imported fabric that signified the prosperity of Venice as a commercial center. Bellini reproduced the effect by painting the surface roughly in order to catch the light.

Bellini influenced the course of European painting through the young painters apprenticed to his workshop. Two of the most famous were Giorgione and **Titian**, whose later rivalry he took in his stride. On a visit to Venice in 1505, Dürer reported, "he is very old and still he is the best painter of them all."

Madonna of the Meadow (c.1505)

Bellini's Madonnas were virtually his trademark, as was the serenity and tenderness with which he portrayed them. Here the child Jesus sleeps blissfully under his mother's gaze while daily life goes on behind them in one of the artist's exquisite landscapes. Only the brooding raven and the solemn pose of the Virgin hint at the day on Calvary, when this same son will lie dead in her lap.

Hieronymus Bosch

Timeline

1450(?) Born Hieronymus an Aken in 's-Hertogenbosch, Netherlands, son of a painter

1480(?) Marries Aleyt Goyaerts van de Merveen

1486 Joins Brotherhood of Our Lady

1504 *Last Judgment* commissioned by Philip I of Spain

1516 Dies in 's-Hertogenbosch

Hieronymus Bosch cannot be categorized. He links back to the miniature narratives depicted on illuminated manuscripts at the same time as anticipating the pots and pans of Dutch genre painting. His family were lay members of the Brotherhood of Our Lady in 's-Hertogenbosch. This Catholic group worked for the cultural benefit of the city where Bosch lived and died.

Bosch's unbridled imagination explodes as he depicts life as a continual struggle between man and his inner nature. There are many theories about his astonishing vision, one of the most persistent being that his symbolism encodes the doctrines of a heretical Gnostic sect called the Cathars, which flourished in the twelfth and thirteenth centuries. Whatever Bosch believed, he had an acute awareness of human psychology. He uses familiar proverbs and folklore to comment on the human condition. His observations—spread across thousands of individual figures in the teeming panels of his triptychs—are continually surfacing, as if to admonish the viewer or proclaim a revelation, and then diving again into the tumult. Bosch painted *alla prima*—that is, directly onto a ground with no underpainting or glazes, a method that called for expert brushwork.

The register that records his death describes Bosch as a "distinguished painter." He was certainly a strong influence on **Bruegel the Elder** and his allegories of village life. Later, Bosch's paintings were avidly collected by Philip II of Spain, before the Protestant Reformation finally dismissed him to obscurity.

King Gaspard, Adoration of the Magi

(detail) (1510)

Bosch's later works depicted fewer and larger figures playing out a single event. Gaspard is one of the Magi in Bosch's version of the Adoration. Behind him, his page wears a bizarre thorny headdress, symbolic of the only crown that Christ will ever wear.

The Garden of Earthly Delights *(c.1500)*

One of the best known of Bosch's paintings, this is the center panel of a huge panoramic triptych. The composition is masterful in the way he manipulates the picture-plane between the viewer and different levels of activity in the picture. Arguments continue over Bosch's intentions with this work, between those who believe it shows a world engaged in sinful pleasures and those who think it is how humanity might have lived without the Fall of Adam and Eve.

15

Sandro Botticelli

Timeline

During his life, Botticelli was connected with three major philosophies. His early pictures are standard Madonnas, made for guilds and private clients. However, Botticelli's relationship with conventional Christianity underwent radical adjustment when he won the patronage of Florentine ruler Lorenzo de' Medici.

De' Medici advocated humanism through the NeoPlatonists, the scholarly group of men he collected around him. Their aim was to marry classical philosophy with Christianity for an entirely new view of the universe; one where paganism was respected and allegory taught life's lessons. This period yielded Botticelli's celebrated "pagan" works, *The Birth of Venus* and *Primavera*.

Everything changed again in 1491, following the death of Lorenzo. Girolamo Savonarola, fanatical vicar-general of the Dominicans, arrived to claim Florence back for Christ. Savonarola instituted the infamous "Bonfires of the Vanities" and Botticelli, now one of his followers, obediently threw several of his own drawings and paintings into the flames. The remaining pictures of his career are noticeably more sober in tone.

Botticelli's most famous pupil was Filippino Lippi, son of Fra Filippo.

Primavera *(detail) (c.1478)*

The grace, coloring, and draperies of the Flora figure were learned from Filippo Lippi. Botticelli's early talent for drawing was probably fostered by the Pollaiuolo brothers, whose work as goldsmiths and engravers required draftsmanship of a high order.

The Mystic Nativity *(1500)*

*The inscription referring to the Apocalypse and "troubles of Italy"
is in both Greek and Latin. Botticelli has used an archaic device
that magnifies the Virgin and Child; altogether, the picture is
calling for a return to medieval morality.*

Sandro Botticelli

Pieter Bruegel the Elder

Timeline

A remarkable fact about Pieter Bruegel the Elder is that after traveling extensively in Italy he returned home to then resume his work in an unaltered Flemish style. His Italian sketchbooks were full of the grandeur of the Alps rather than copies of Renaissance art.

Bruegel the Elder was nicknamed "Peasant" because he liked to go in disguise among ordinary working people. He was actually one of a group of distinguished Flemish humanists, which included the geographer Ortelius, also Plantin the printer, and Goltzius the engraver, so it would be a mistake to confuse him with one of his peasant figures.

He began painting comparatively late; *Proverbs* dates from 1558. It set a pattern for combining realism and imagination, doubtless inspired by **Bosch**. Similarly, Bruegel's characters often point to morals and make satirical observations on life, although Bruegel's approach is rather more gentle than Bosch's.

Three robust exceptions are *The Fall of the Rebel Angels*, *The Triumph of Death,* and *Mad Meg* (Dulle Griet). In fact, the first nightmarish image was attributed to Bosch until reframing revealed Bruegel's signature. His vengeful *Mad Meg* may be a reference to the terrors of the Spanish Inquisition.

Bruegel made social and political protests as readily as he celebrated the joys of living. In painting he found a vital means of expressing his inner and outer vision: "In all my works there was more thought than painting."

Parable of the Blind *(detail) (1568)*

A detail from Bruegel's last major work, referring to a quotation from Matthew's gospel: "If the blind lead the blind, both shall fall into the ditch." In this solemn allegory for the human situation, the string of unfortunate people, each by clinging blindly to the next, are jeopardizing their own salvation rather than working it out for themselves.

Children's Games *(1560)*

Bruegel's skill with genre scenes such as this one, depicting hundreds of little people acting out a catalog of pastimes, was honed while he was an engraver with the Antwerp publisher Hieronymus Cock. His figures are solid with little modeling but they are wonderfully lively; and beyond the fascination of identifying all the games and activities, the viewer is treated to a convincing street perspective on the right, and a delightful glimpse of typical Flemish landscape on the left.

Antonio Canaletto

Antonio Canaletto chose to paint his native city, Venice, knowing it could make him plenty of money. His formula—masses of detailed architecture, shimmering waters, and blue skies—went down well with the English nobility undertaking the Grand Tour. So well that, at one stage, Joseph Smith, the British consul-in-waiting, was acting as his agent.

Over time, Canaletto refined his output to suit the market even better. His repertoire grew to include popular Venetian festivals and ceremonies and he was willing to paint an entire series of *vedute* (city views) in a uniform size, to furnish any stately home.

Canaletto made no secret of his reliance on the *camera obscura* (see page 116 for a definition of this device), especially at sketchbook stage. The camera itself was well known, and first recorded in 1550. Canaletto taught others how to use it and thus render perspective convincingly. His nephew, Bernardo Bellotto, proved an excellent pupil and eventually painted for crowned heads all over Europe.

In 1740, war broke out in Europe and disrupted foreign travel. It was a time to seek out English clients at home. In 1746, Canaletto moved to London, where he lived for almost ten years, working for patrons such as the Hanoverian duke of Richmond.

Eton College (c.1754)

This view of the famous English public school near Windsor was painted toward the end of Canaletto's stay in England, which had begun in 1746.

Canaletto's most fervent patron, Joseph Smith, sold much of his collection to King George III in 1762, thereby forming the majority of the paintings by Canaletto owned by the Royal Collection at Windsor Castle in England.

Basin of St. Mark's Square, Venice *(detail) (c.1745?)*

The view that so many Grand Tourists traveled to see, and buy—on canvas. It was not unknown for enthusiastic clients to take their Canalettos home before the paint had dried.

Michelangelo Merisi da Caravaggio

Caravaggio's early education in Lombardy gave him a passion for realism and a dislike of idealization; later, in Rome, he would discover that these were revolutionary concepts. The models chosen for saints and supplicants in his religious pictures were genuine peasants with rags, wrinkles, and dirty feet. Not surprisingly, this upset orthodox patrons and members of the public alike, who preferred the contrived elegance of Mannerism to Caravaggio's down-to-earth observation.

Caravaggio himself very much admired **Michelangelo** Buonarroti and paid homage to him several times. The angel's hands in *The Inspiration of St. Matthew*, painted for the Contarelli Chapel, recalls *God's Creation of Adam* on the Sistine Chapel ceiling; and in *St. John the Baptist (Youth with Ram)*, the boy poses exactly like one of the *ignudi*, also on the Sistine ceiling.

It appears that Caravaggio's method was to paint directly from his models, with no preparatory drawing. This indicates the use of lenses as a technical aid. His patron, Cardinal del Monte, is known to have had some expertise with optics and may have provided the artist with equipment that would have projected the images directly onto the canvas, helping to reproduce points of high contrast and foreshortening.

Boy With a Basket of Fruit

(1593–4)

The boy, who looks as if he could be offering himself to the viewer along with the fruit, is possibly a self-portrait. Caravaggio would have been around twenty-one years of age but already demonstrated an assurance in handling the extremes of light and shadow known as chiaroscuro.

The Supper at Emmaus *(detail) (1596–1602)*

The gestures in this picture tell us a great deal. The outstretched hands of the disciple on the right, and those of the other gripping his chair, capture the immediate moment of recognition, as the beardless youth they met along the road reveals himself to be the resurrected Christ by blessing the meal. The still life of fruit makes biblical references to restored life and expectations fulfilled, while the apples—symbols of temptation—remain noticeably blighted.

By upholding his own aesthetic values and avoiding any consolatory approach to his subjects, Caravaggio quite literally placed art in a new light. The fresh immediacy of his work suited the aims of the Catholic Counter-Reformation too, as they hoped that dramatic imagery in their churches could be used to tempt people back from dour Protestantism.

Caravaggio combined a short, wild, occasionally criminal life with an iconoclastic attitude. His influence lived on in the studios of the Gentileschi family, particularly that of the remarkably talented Artemisia Gentileschi. Caravaggio's works continue to resonate, specifically with film-makers such as Pasolini, Jarman, and Bertolucci.

Paul Cézanne

Timeline

1839 Born in Aix-en-Provence, France, son of a banker.

1852–9 Studies at Collège Bourbon with Emile Zola.

1859–61 Studies law at Aix.

1861 Studies art in Paris, returns to Aix.

1862–70 Rejected by Paris Salon. Franco-Prussian war drives him to l'Estaque. Meets Hortense Fiquet.

1872 Birth of son Paul.

1873–79 In Pontoise and Auvers-sur-Oise with Pissarro.

1880–88 Lives in l'Estaque and later moves to Gardanne.

1886 Marries Hortense. Father dies leaving him an inheritance.

1895 First one-man show at Ambroise Vollard Gallery, Paris.

1906 Dies of pneumonia in Aix.

Still Life with Pots and Fruit *(1890–94)*

A study of shape, volume, and color, all minutely arranged, to illustrate perfectly Cézanne's own words: "Treat nature by means of the cylinder, the sphere, the cone, everything brought into proper perspective … directed toward a central point."

Paul Cézanne was a shy, irritable man who, after a discouraging start in the early 1860s—a forbidding father, examination failure, and Salon refusals—scarcely seemed destined for lasting recognition. Acclaim was hard won, taking over thirty years of disciplined work before his first one-man exhibition in 1895; following which, younger artists like the Nabis formed an enthusiastic clique, alert to Cézanne's pushing of the boundaries beyond airy Impressionism.

Cézanne knew that the theories of Parisian academics and critics, let alone public opinion, were not sympathetic to his ideal of "the logical development of everything we see and feel through the study of nature." It was his desire for this essential harmony, expressed by color as tone, that drew him back to his beloved Provence in 1882. The recluse who wished "to make of Impressionism something solid and durable" eventually went much further, providing the impetus for Cubism, Abstraction, and the gamut of avant-garde experimentation.

Renoir asked: "How on earth does he do it? He cannot put two touches of color on to a canvas without its being already an achievement."

In the Park of Chateau Noir (c.1895)
Cézanne's landscapes of this period were solidly built from planes of color, but "modulation" was always Cézanne's keyword and he worked patches of subtle earth hues coherently alongside stronger tones of green and blue for a supremely imaginative evocation of his native countryside.

John Constable

Timeline

John Constable based his paintings on sketches done outdoors, directly from nature. As a student he had dutifully copied the landscapes of Van Ruisdael and other masters but—although he admired them greatly—he refused to create work in the same style, saying, "It would be dishonest to wear Claude's coat and call it mine." He was referring to Claude Lorrain (1600–82), a landscape painter whose work inspired him.

Constable's method depended on using "divided tones" (pure colors juxtaposed to recreate the vibrancy of external light) laid on with rapid brushstrokes. Such a daringly original approach was criticized by the English Academy but acclaimed by the French. It was Paris that gave Constable due recognition—and a gold medal—when *The Haywain* was exhibited in 1824. Delacroix and Géricault became instant devotees of his Romantic naturalism.

The Haywain came from Constable's London studio, where he had lived since his marriage in 1816. All the pictures that he painted there relied on skillful preparation from full-size sketches, and many of the canvases were "six-footers." Only when Constable had pieced together a sketch in sufficient detail to refresh his memory was he prepared to begin work.

Sadly, few bought Constable's work in his lifetime, forcing him to rely on the generosity of others. His long-awaited admission to the Royal Academy came in 1829, after years of failure to acknowledge his dedication to interpreting the mutability of landscape; and just when large swathes of it were being swallowed up by the industrial revolution.

Study of Sky and Trees

For Constable, "skying" meant making small oil studies of clouds, with full notes written on the back. Typically, he covered red primer in thick strokes and overlapping colors, which gave depth to the cloud formation. They were not necessarily part of any larger composition, but recorded the reality of weather, light, and color in a particular patch of sky.

The Cornfield *(1826)*

The inhabited landscape was Constable's constant and most intimate theme. The lane to the cornfield is the same one the artist followed to school; this is the Suffolk that he carried in his heart all his life. The Cornfield traces several points in time and space. The vertical format steers the viewer's gaze, from the boy at the stream, to the man reaping the corn, and finally, to the church tower among the trees. The Romantic poet Wordsworth subscribed to the fund that purchased this picture for the English National Gallery.

Salvador Dalí

Salvador Dalí was an irrepressible self-publicist and the cultivator of the art world's most famous mustache. The technical brilliance with which he could paint and draw gave him equal facility for reproducing various styles, from Realism, Impressionism, and Cubism to the *Metafisica* of the Italians de Chirico and Carra. His versatility and skills also extended to sculpture and film-making.

The screenplay he wrote for Buñuel's *Un Chien Andalou* admitted Dalí to the Surrealists' group when he moved to Paris in 1928. This coincided with his discovery of Freud's theory of the unconscious; reading *The Interpretation of Dreams* led to Dalí's emphasis on dream imagery and his "paranoiac-critical" method. However, the artist's right-wing political views caused an eventual split with the Surrealists.

As war loomed in 1939, Dalí and Gala left Europe for the United States, returning to Spain in 1948. Dalí's fame was always controversial, thanks to his provocative exhibitionism as much as to the media. Yet in his own lifetime, his popularity supported two museums dedicated exclusively to his works.

Dalí's introduction to Cubism and the art of collage came about through a fellow Spaniard, Juan Gris (1887–1927). He was the most able practitioner of Cubism and evolved an individual approach through meticulous grid drawings (he had originally studied engineering). On arriving in Paris in 1906, he settled among **Picasso**'s circle in Montmartre, which included Apollinaire, and was championed by the writer Gertrude Stein. In later years, Diaghilev commissioned him to design for the Ballets Russes. Unfortunately, Gris suffered chronic depression and physical illness, which brought about his early death.

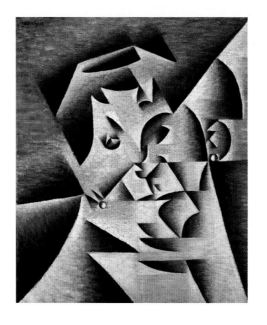

Head (c.1912) by Juan Gris

In the early "analytic" phase of Cubism, Gris' palette was coolly limited. Around 1912, his tones grew richer and he used russet browns and creamy whites. In addition, he would stipple the surface in certain areas, all of which marked his movement toward Cubism's "synthetic" phase.

Invisible Afghan with Apparition on Beach of Face of Garcia in Form of Fruit Dish with Three Figs *(1938)* by Salvador Dalí

The "paranoiac-critical" method used in Dalí's "hand-painted dream photographs" involved perceiving more than one image in a configuration. The dominant image here is the face constructed from an urn and two men's heads; the figs are formed by the rocks beyond; and the outline of the Afghan hound takes shape through windswept clouds, its head resting on the cliffs and its paws on the sand. Dalí's friend, the poet Lorca, had been killed in the Spanish Civil War in 1936 and this may explain his "apparition."

Jacques-Louis David

Timeline

When Jacques-Louis David returned to France from Italy in 1780, it was with strong ideals based on the supposed virtues of ancient Rome. He was committed to Neoclassicism, which demanded that artists should take their subjects and style from antique models, as Poussin had 150 years previously. The French responded by electing David to both the Academy and the Salon. His highly finished line, color, and composition were greatly admired. More than that, his style was perceived as revolutionary, matching the country's mood for an end to aristocratic corruption and a return to the stern, patriotic morals of republican Rome.

Upon joining the revolutionary Convention, David voted for Louis XVI's execution. But on the death of Robespierre and the end of the Reign of Terror, he was jailed and might have been executed too, had his royalist wife not intervened with the new "emperor," Napoléon Bonaparte.

David became a devoted follower of Napoléon. He found himself at the height of his influence and gained a knighthood in the new Legion of Honour.

Exiled to Brussels after Napoléon's fall from power in 1816, David—an outstanding teacher—continued to train young painters, including Ingres (1780–1867). He was the virtual art dictator of France for a generation; his influence spread to fashion, furniture design, and interiors, and found echoes in the development of moral philosophy.

Napoléon Bonaparte Crossing the Alps *(1801)*

This lively propaganda portrait was copied no fewer than four times by David and his studio. The message suggested is that if Napoléon can attack the Alps with such vigor, then he will stop at nothing.

The Death of Marat *(detail) (1793)*

This is David's greatest work and a supreme example of political painting. The radical revolutionary Marat is shown just after Charlotte Corday—a Girondist—has tricked her way in, with the note that he is still holding, and stabbed him in his bath. The immense dark space above Marat's head emphasizes the void that he has left, both in the Jacobin cause and in the life of his friend David. The Death of Marat has often been compared with Michelangelo's Pietà; it is an image of secular martyrdom.

Edgar Degas

Timeline

Edgar Degas' personal wealth gave him freedom to devote himself to art. He shunned formal training, preferring to study the Renaissance through frequent trips to Italy and—on his own doorstep—copying in the Louvre. There, in 1862, he and **Manet** met in front of a Velázquez. Degas, who never ceased investigating every technical aspect of painting and drawing, had spent three years on the basics of light and color. Manet may or may not have suggested a new approach to him but, at any rate, he did introduce Degas to the future Impressionists. Degas exhibited with them right from the start in 1874, although he never wholly accepted their doctrines or techniques for himself. He only signed his works when he sold or exhibited them, thus controlling their number and value in the marketplace.

His subjects come from his own background: the high-born fraternity of the racecourse and opera house; ballet rehearsals attended as a privileged visitor; and the nudes seemingly observed, as he said himself, "through the keyhole." Degas was also captivated by Japanese prints, which inspired him to experiment with oblique and unusual perspectives.

The Opera Orchestra *(1868–9)*

The first of a series of canvases featuring orchestral musicians, this is a portrait of Degas' friend Désiré Dihau, democratically placed among other members of the orchestra just below a bright frieze of dancers in the stage footlights. The work is relatively early and hints at Ingres and Delacroix, both admired by Degas. Degas and Delacroix had a scientific interest in color theory and pigments.

The Laundresses *(c. 1884)*

Nothing could be much further from the glamor of the Opera
than the toil of two weary laundresses, but the strong diagonal
of the ironing table is reminiscent of the edge of the stage.
His other inspiration for this picture was the realism of
Daumier's portrayal of working life. Degas counted almost
two thousand Daumier prints among his private art collection.

Unfortunately, Degas' caustic wit lost him many friends and he came to a solitary old age. Yet his biggest problem was always his failing eyesight. Perhaps that was why he took up photography at the age of sixty-one, the camera being effectively a new pair of eyes. His expert venture into pastels was another attempt to work around the problem. But his last resort was to make small wax sculptures of dancers and horses: "…one sees no longer except in memory."

Eugène Delacroix

Timeline

Women of Algiers *(detail) (1834)*

In 1832 Delacroix was with the French Ambassador's retinue on a visit to the Sultan of Morocco, and he often drew on the experience for inspiration. This detail displays the technique he adopted after observing Constable's use of "divided color" and its vibrant effects.

Eugène Delacroix prided himself on the speed at which he could work: "skillful enough to sketch a man falling out of a window during the time it takes him to get…to the ground." And not only did he paint, he loved music, read widely, and wrote fascinating letters and journals about his life and times.

Delacroix studied with Géricault (1791–1824) under Guerin and subsequently posed for his friend as the prone figure on the *Raft of the Medusa*. The picture provided impetus to Delacroix's own creativity but he never accepted the Romantic label, obstinately insisting that he was "a pure classicist." He greatly admired and copied Michelangelo, **Veronese**, and **Rubens** in the Louvre, and always made very careful preparatory drawings.

Delacroix's political masterpiece, *Liberty Leading the People,* is an allegory painted in the wake of the 1830 Paris revolution. He included himself beside the iconic Liberty figure as the armed man in the top hat.

Delacroix had completed the journey from startling, innovative colorist to respected older artist by the time he came to influence modern masters, like **Cézanne**, **Degas**, **Van Gogh**, and **Picasso**. As long as he lived he was, as the poet Baudelaire wrote, "passionately in love with passion, and coldly determined to seek the means to express passion in the manner visible."

Massacre at Chios *(detail) (1824)*

Inspired by Géricault's treatment of the theme of suffering, Delacroix presents a harrowing scene from the Greek rebellion against the Turks, which roused many Europeans (including Byron) to their cause. The painting was bought at the Salon of 1824 by the French government, perhaps by Talleyrand in covert support of his son. Significantly, at the same Salon, Delacroix encountered Constable's Haywain.

Albrecht Dürer

Timeline

Albrecht Dürer was the foremost artist of the Northern Renaissance. He came from Nuremberg, usefully situated halfway between the Netherlands and Italy, which enabled him to travel with ease in either direction. The notion of "Renaissance man" appealed to Dürer, whose self-portraits—a new idea in itself—stamped his image on the developing European tradition.

After a visit to Venice in 1494, he remained in Nuremberg for the next ten years, busy producing woodcuts and engravings that marked him as one of the major printmakers of all time. His prints were distributed throughout Europe—bearing his distinctive "AD" monogram—and his fame was assured wherever he went.

Despite complaining that oil painting took up more time than it was financially worth, Dürer painted numerous altarpieces and portraits. In time, he allied himself to the ideas of the Reformation, and there was a blending of northern realism with the Renaissance vision.

Dürer conserved his works on paper, sometimes dated and even with notes on the subject matter. His words have survived too, in letters and diaries, and also in the *Course on the Art of Measuring*, one of the first books on the use of mathematics in art, a true Renaissance topic.

Self-Portrait *(1498)*

The composition of this panel portrait follows the Florentine style. In it, the clothes, hairstyle, and distant view of snow-topped mountains all indicate that Dürer considered himself a dignified man of the world, and no mere provincial craftsman.

Four Horsemen of the Apocalypse *(1498)* (opposite)

Dürer realized that prints made his art available to the widest possible public and hired an agent to sell them in the fairs and markets of Europe. The Apocalypse was Dürer's earliest major series, illustrating the Book of Revelation *with the Scripture on the reverse. His interpretation of the four horsemen—War, Famine, Pestilence, and Death—has never been surpassed.*

Caspar David Friedrich

Timeline

1774	Born in Greifswald, Germany, son of a candle-maker.
1794–98	Studies at Academy of Copenhagen.
1798	Settles in Dresden.
1805	Awarded prize by Weimar Friends of Art.
1807	Begins work in oils.
1811	Becomes member of Berlin Academy.
1816	Enters Dresden Academy.
1818	Marries Caroline Bommer in Dresden.
1824	Becomes assistant professor at Dresden Academy.
1835	Suffers a stroke but continues to work in sepia and watercolor.
1840	Dies in Dresden.

Caspar David Friedrich studied painting and natural history in Copenhagen but eventually chose to live in Dresden, whose beautiful surroundings inspired so many of his mystic landscapes. Dresden was also the hub of the Romantic movement in Germany and not only did Friedrich make the acquaintance of painter Philipp Otto Runge, but also met several poets there, including Goethe.

For nine years, he worked only in pencil or sepia, his subjects ranging from seascapes to mountains, often at certain times of day or changes of season. A switch to oil paints boosted his creativity and in 1807 he caused a sensation with *Cross in the Mountains*. Designed for a private chapel, Friedrich's landscape evoked the spirit of the Crucifixion. Shocked by his use of a secular scene to convey a religious message, several critics went as far as accusing him of sacrilege.

Although Friedrich tried both portrait work and architecture, he always returned to landscapes, where he could paint ruined churches and lonely figures in vast spaces, often bathed in a symbolic light. Friedrich suffered a stroke in 1835 and was limited from then onward to sepia sketches and watercolors. His immediate influence was confined to a few students, but his work was rediscovered at the end of the century.

Wanderer Above the Sea of Fog *(1818)* (opposite)
The wild-haired, solitary figure is Friedrich himself, who, in the character of the Wanderer—booted and stick in hand—has climbed a rocky peak above the mountain mists. Only a short time ahead of the American "sublime" artists, Friedrich has located his God in Nature. The dark contrast between the rock and the swirling white fog also makes this an awesome prospect for the viewer.

The Riesengebirge *(1830–4)*
Painted during a period of happy stability in his life, Friedrich looks back on a mountain tour he made twenty years earlier and recollects a panorama of tranquility. Here the sky meets the horizon in a blend of soft yellow and violet, a muted contrast that is echoed in the delicate cloud studies above.

Thomas Gainsborough

Timeline

Thomas Gainsborough was a founding member of London's Royal Academy, together with Joshua Reynolds. Both were accomplished portrait painters but Reynolds modeled himself on **Rembrandt**, whereas Gainsborough, having first studied Watteau and Van Ruisdael, became a dedicated admirer of **Van Dyck**.

Like many artists, Gainsborough submitted to the tyranny of society portraiture. He wrote to a friend whose wife's portrait he had already begun: "I have no oftener promised myself the Pleasure of sitting down to [finish] it but some confounded ugly creature or other have pop'd their Heads in my way and hindred me."

His remarkable ability to achieve a likeness with spontaneity and freshness had been legendary since boyhood. Furthermore, Gainsborough could render any texture of fabric, from muslin to satin. However, he preferred landscape painting to portraits and hit upon the happy combination of posing clients on their country estates, which also allowed him to view their art collections.

Gainsborough's move to London in 1774 attracted the attention of George III. Liking his informality and Tory sympathies, the king asked him to paint the royal family, bypassing the official Court painter, Joshua Reynolds. The old rivals were reconciled at Gainsborough's final illness, when he famously cried from his bed: "We are all going to Heaven and Van Dyck is of the company."

The Blue Boy *(1770) (opposite)*

By dressing the boy, Jonathan Buttall, the son of a friend, in a suit of satin, Gainsborough is paying homage to Van Dyck; and by making the suit blue, he is challenging Reynolds who declared that "the main mass of a picture could not be blue."

The Harvest Wagon *(1767)*

Confined to town, Gainsborough often drew candle-lit model landscapes set up in his studio. He came to appreciate Rubens and the Dutch master's influence can be detected here, in the fluency of line and the scale of the beech trees. The group on the cart may be based on Rubens'
Descent from the Cross.

Giotto di Bondone

Timeline

1267	Born in Vespignano, Italy.
1277	Reputedly discovered by Florentine painter Giovanni Cimabue.
1300	Works in Rome on fresco for Lateran Palace.
1305–06	Paints frescoes in Arena Chapel, Padua.
1311–20(?)	Paints frescoes in Assisi, Padua, and Rimini.
1321–30(?)	Works in Florence.
1334	Appointed architect and master of works for cathedral and city of Florence.
1335–36	Works in Milan.
1337	Dies in Florence.

When Giotto was a shepherd boy he was reputedly discovered by his master Giovanni Cimabue scratching the picture of a sheep on a rock. From then on, western art followed a new course. The boy probably worked first on mosaics in the Florentine Baptistery before his interests spread to painting, sculpture, and architecture. Giotto became a successful businessman as well, running a busy workshop and supporting eight children.

However—prosperous or not—Giotto's contribution would have been immeasurable. Cimabue had worked to represent form in its own space, but it was Giotto who finally discarded Byzantine tradition and, in imitation of nobody, took the portrayal of humanity to new levels. There is an authenticity of expression in the eyes of his figures and every gesture is convincing because real bodies inhabit their clothing.

It seems no expense was spared with costly ultramarine pigment for painting the Arena Chapel in Padua. The glorious blue later inspired Proust to describe the effect as "radiant day." There is so much of the outdoors in Giotto's work that it would be surprising if he had not spent his childhood in the countryside. And he makes us feel there is such a thing as inner space, too; we are encouraged to respond emotionally to every detail of his dramatic narrative.

Giotto passed on his mastery of fresco painting directly to his pupils. Almost a century later, his work inspired Masaccio (1401–28/9) and later still, **Michelangelo** was busy studying his legacy.

Jesus Before the High Priest Caiphas *(1305–06)*
South Wall, Arena Chapel, Padua
Giotto makes the beamed ceiling of Caiphas' chamber look like the lid of a strongbox, it is obvious there is no escape. So much activity jostles for space that it takes a moment to pick out Jesus' sorrowful glance toward a half-hidden Peter, who has just denied being one of his disciples.

The Resurrection of Lazarus *(1305–06)*

North Wall, Arena Chapel, Padua

Lazarus, the brother of Martha and Mary, has been dead four days. His sisters have wisely covered their noses and mouths while the tomb is opened and Jesus miraculously restores him to life. Giotto has placed Jesus and Lazarus in such a way as to mirror each other, the message being that before long Jesus will die and undergo a resurrection too.

43

El Greco

Timeline

When El Greco (Domenikos Theotokopoulos) the icon painter left Crete for Venice, he was confronted—quite literally—by new perspectives. His first major influence was **Titian**; Bassano was another. However, there are strong indications that El Greco actually worked under Tintoretto. Both artists made compositional sketches from clay or wax statuettes, artificially lit. And Tintoretto's influence shines through in El Greco's *Christ Driving the Traders From the Temple*.

In Rome, El Greco had little success, perhaps due to his arrogant claim that he could paint better than **Michelangelo**. Proud and self-assertive, he later became embroiled in long-term lawsuits. The nickname "Greco" irked him as well and he always signed his work Domenikos Theotokopoulos in Greek, sometimes adding Kres ("Cretan"). Nevertheless, while in Rome he consolidated the "essence of Byzantium" with Italian Mannerism. He compressed space and twisted his forms and may well have used lenses and mirrors to develop these effects.

Although Toledo demanded a cooler palette, the move to Spain did not diminish El Greco's religious and mystical intensity. Spain's key Catholic city engaged with the Counter-Reformation by investing generously in religious art, and the formality of Spanish altarpieces offered tall, narrow panels to complement the artist's elongated figures.

El Greco's unique style had no followers and was disregarded for centuries. A group of art lovers rediscovered him in the nineteenth century, to the admiration of artists such as **Delacroix**, **Degas**, **Cézanne**, **Van Gogh**, and Gauguin (1848–1903).

St Louis IX of France *(1586–94)*

Louis IX, king of France, was canonized in 1297 as the ideal Christian monarch. El Greco painted him for the Counter-Reformation cause. Although the face is traditionally iconic with high cheekbones and staring dark eyes, El Greco places Louis' body in the fashionable three-quarter pose and gives him beautifully expressive hands.

View of Toledo *(detail) (1597–99)*

In the ancient city of Toledo, immortalized here in one of the earliest and most dramatic landscapes in western art, El Greco found a sympathetic circle of intellectual friends and patrons and built a profitable career.

Matthias Grünewald

Timeline

1470(?) Born Mathis Neithardt
Gothart in Wurzburg,
Germany.

1480(?) Apprenticed to a
goldsmith in Strasbourg,
later works in Colmar in
Schongauer's studio.

1490–98 Works in Basel as
woodcut illustrator.

1501–21 Proprietor of workshop
in Seligenstadt.

1503 Earliest known work,
Mocking of Christ.

1511–26 Works at court of
Archbishop of Mainz.

1512–15 Paints *Isenheim Altarpiece*
for hospital chapel of
St Anthony's Monastery
in Alsace.

1514 Meets Dürer.

1525 Embraces Lutherism.
Flees to Halle, works as
hydraulic engineer.

1528 Dies of the plague in Halle.

A contemporary of Bosch, Cranach (1472–1553), and **Dürer**, Matthias Grünewald considered his own reputation secondary to the religious and social message of his paintings.

From 1511, Grünewald was employed by the archbishops of Mainz as a Court painter. It was the era of the Reformation and the artist's sympathies lay with the Protestant cause, but he managed to keep his secret until he disclosed his support for the Peasant's Revolt in 1525. He was dismissed, and from then on embraced Lutherism, exchanging painting for a career as a hydraulic engineer.

Grünewald is seen nowadays as the great precursor of twentieth-century German Expressionism, but this was not realized until Modernism prompted a reevaluation of his work as an alternative to classical idealism. Grünewald himself did not seek to uncover any great artistic truths or to break new ground with his style. What he did was for the plain understanding of those sufferers and their carers who knelt in front of the altars that he had decorated. His images, whether sorrowful or triumphant, and his extraordinary use of color surpass the need for words.

St Anthony of Egypt's Visit to St. Paul the Hermit,

Isenheim Altarpiece *(detail) (c.1515)* (opposite)

This story would have been familiar to everyone who prayed in the chapel of St. Anthony's Hospitallers in Isenheim. The old hermit tells their patron saint about the raven who has miraculously fed him with half a loaf of bread every day for sixty years. The bird was doubly obliging that day and brought a ration for St. Anthony too.

Crucifixion, Isenheim Altarpiece

(center panel) (c.1515)

The Hospitallers cared for victims of incurable diseases such as St Anthony's Fire (ergotism), so this image of torment and pain would have made a consoling link between Christ and the sick. The words of the inscription: "He must increase but I must decrease" are emphasized by the disproportionate sizes of Jesus and those gathered around the cross.

Ando Hiroshige

Timeline

1797	Born in Edo, Japan, son of a fire warden.
1811–12	Pupil of book illustrator Utagawa Toyohiro.
1811–30	Creates prints of traditional subjects, including views of Edo.
1834	Publishes complete edition *Fifty-three Stations of the Tokaido Road.*
1833–40	Peak of popularity, publishes various notable series.
1841–43	Tempo Era austerity affects quality of work.
1855	Abandons horizontal format for vertical.
1858	Dies of cholera.

Ando Hiroshige was a leading exponent of *ukiyo-e*—"pictures of the floating world"—during the last half-century of its existence as a Japanese art form. Ukiyo-e originated in the late seventeenth century, dedicated to the pursuit of pleasure in everyday urban life and based on popular idols taken from the ranks of courtesans and actors.

The collectable ukiyo-e woodblock prints developed along relatively sophisticated lines of their own, within a Japanese tradition of harmonious color and graceful composition, which raised them above plain folk art. They were priced to suit the pockets of middle-class tradesmen, artisans, and merchants. Paintings were reserved for the wealthier ranks.

Hiroshige's total output was immense, some 5,400 prints. He studied drawing from childhood and was apprenticed to just one master, Utagawa Toyohiro. Yet Hiroshige worked for over twenty years before producing the series that established his reputation, *Fifty-three Stations of the Tokaido Road*; an ambitious travelog that followed the great highway between Kyoto and Edo.

Working in the nineteenth century, Hiroshige and **Hokusai** each preferred to create landscapes rather than portraits of actors, wrestlers, poets, and courtesans. The innate love of the Japanese for all aspects of the natural world ensured that both artists had an enthusiastic following. Although he may not have matched Hokusai's draftsmanship, Hiroshige at his best is unsurpassed in his poetic vision. His ability to evoke the mood of a particular place still has unfailing appeal to westerners.

Rice Planting in the Rain at Ono,
Hoki Province *(c. 1855)*

Hiroshige was not afraid to use western-style perspective; here the rice fields stretch away to the foot of a mist-covered hill. Meanwhile, rain-drenched workers plant up reflective squares of water with shoots of rice, in a beautifully modulated patchwork of greens and grays.

Night Snow at Kanbara *(1832–34)*

A woodblock from the series Fifty-three Stations of the Tokaido Road. *His characteristically shaded sky registers twilight over a mountain village engulfed in snow, through which three people are struggling home. Snow, rain, or mist are favored background conditions against which Hiroshige sets his travelers, often depicted crossing each others' paths, emphasizing the transience of existence.*

David Hockney

Timeline

1937 Born in Bradford, England, son of a clerk.

1953–57 Studies at Bradford School of Art.

1959–62 Studies at Royal College of Art, London; meets Kitaj.

1963 Publishes *Rake's Progress* etchings. First visit to North Africa. Meets Andy Warhol in New York.

1964–68 Travels, paints, teaches, and exhibits across U.S.A.

1970 Retrospective at Whitechapel Gallery, London; tours Europe.

1973 Moves to Paris.

1978 Settles in Los Angeles.

1982 Takes up photography.

1984 Resumes painting after three-year break. Begins series of lithographs.

1988 Major retrospective shown in U.S.A. and U.K. Sets up studio in Malibu.

1995–96 Major retrospective of drawings, Royal Academy, London.

2005 Exhibits watercolors of East Yorkshire landscape.

David Hockney is one of most versatile artists of his generation, many of whom have not developed as interestingly from their common roots in Pop Art. Throughout a long career, Hockney has managed both to court controversy and to become a British national treasure, as witnessed by his creation as a Freeman of Bradford, his hometown. He has maintained strong ties with Yorkshire and recently returned to make gentle watercolors of the landscape. These exist in total contrast to his monumental treatment of the Grand Canyon, originally exhibited at London's Royal Academy.

Not only is Hockney a skilled draftsman, he has also produced etchings to illustrate *Six Fairy Tales of the Brothers Grimm* and C.P. Cavafy's *Poems*. During the 1970s he ventured into stage design with costumes and sets for Stravinsky's *The Rake's Progress* and Mozart's *The Magic Flute*, both staged at Glyndebourne. Many

Scene from The Rake's Progress, *San Francisco 1982*

Hockney first engaged with reinterpreting Hogarth's Rake's Progress *when he embarked on a suite of etchings in 1961.*

In 1975 he designed the set and costumes for Stravinsky's opera version, first performed at the Glyndebourne Festival, England.

Hockney's theater work mixes practicality with exceptional vision. To those who accused him of neglecting painting, he replied: "I've never treated the theatre as a sideline, nothing I do is a sideline."

say that his painting style has benefited from the broadening out that was required for stage design. When Hockney took up photography, he pursued mechanical image-making through various processes, from photographic collage and photocopying to ciglee (inkjet).

The debate continues over his apparent avoidance of subjects such as war, poverty, sickness, and injustice, and whether one can be a great artist without confronting "serious" issues. But Hockney believes it is vital to continue looking and learning, with the dedication of an explorer who suspects there is so much more to discover about art itself.

Mr and Mrs Clark and Percy *(detail) (1970–71)*

Ossie Clark's flowing designs combined with Celia Birtwell's printed textiles produced some of the most desirable garments of the late 1960s and early 1970s. Hockney plays with allusions as if he were a Renaissance portraitist. The lilies associated with Mrs Clark stand for purity and incorruptibility and the cat Percy sits bolt upright on Mr Clark's lap. The couple occupy two distinct halves of the canvas, which could be divided easily enough. This may or may not reflect the fact that the Clarks were divorced within three years.

William Hogarth

Timeline

The Shrimp Girl (c. 1743)

Hogarth kept this lively portrait for himself. It is based on a popular theme known as the Cries of London, *where different street traders were portrayed in a series of prints. This rapidly executed oil sketch, an unusual approach to portraiture, gives the impression of a face glimpsed in passing. Hogarth's widow showed the picture to visitors with the comment: "They said he could not paint flesh. There's flesh and blood for you!"*

Wickedly witty Londoner William Hogarth has at least two claims to fame. First, through his own academy in St. Martin's Lane, he probably did more than any individual to establish an English school of painting. And secondly, he produced forerunners of the graphic novel with several series on "modern morals," the two best known being *A Rake's Progress* and *Marriage A-la-Mode*. Hogarth's great friend Henry Fielding (author of *Tom Jones*) put it perfectly when he called him "a comic literary painter." Through satire, both Fielding and Hogarth exposed the evils of their age, targeting the mean, calculating morality of those who took the poverty and misery of others as stepping stones to their own advantage.

As far as Hogarth was concerned, he was also campaigning against the taste for French Rococo (he was an exact contemporary of Boucher), which he reckoned was undermining the livelihood of English artists. His attitude was not improved by his arrest in Calais for spying, after being caught sketching the port's fortifications.

In 1753, Hogarth published a tract called *The Analysis of Beauty*. This was partly a rebuke aimed at so-called connoisseurs for being insufficiently informed about art; and partly a valuable contribution to the discussion of aesthetics. Hogarth had a theory that a "line of beauty" in the shape of an "S" was intrinsic to the structure of a picture. Looking carefully into the *Painter and his Pug*, we see he has drawn the famous "S" on his palette.

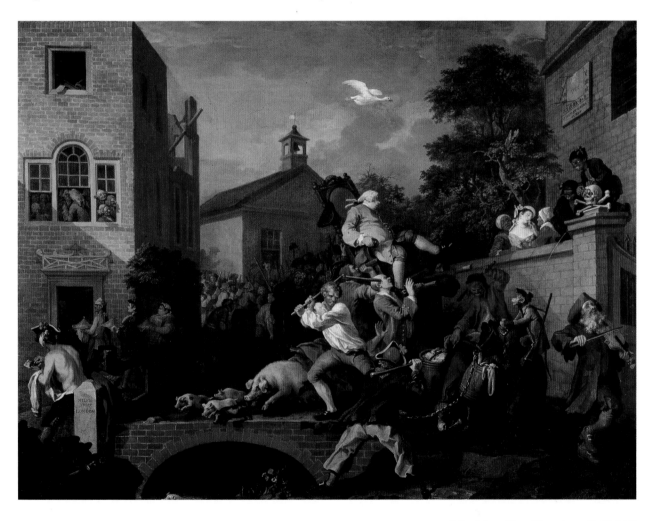

Chairing the Member *(1754/5)*

"An Election" was Hogarth's final modern morals series. Illustrated in four parts, this is the final scene, when everything degenerates into a riot. Hogarth often makes sly references to earlier history paintings within his own; this time it is Charles Le Brun's Victory of Alexander over Darius. *Instead of the imperial eagle signifying victory, Hogarth has a fat goose flying over the head of the new member of parliament. It suggests that his contribution to debate will be no better than that bird's cackling.*

Katsushika Hokusai

The Poetess Ono no Komachi *(c. 1810)*

The poems accompanying ukiyo-e *prints take various forms. Here is an image of the Japanese poetess Ono no Komachi with one of her poems, quoted word for word. The letters of her name are also in the outlines of her figure and the screen.*

Hokusai was responsible for a phenomenal thirty thousand works of art. He lived for nothing else and was driven to perfect his style with every new undertaking. Between the ages of sixty-four and seventy-two he had a burst of creativity that resulted in several major series of woodblock prints, including *The Thirty-six Views of Mount Fuji*.

As a youth, Hokusai was on a constant quest for his artistic niche. After a relatively long period under Katsukawa Shunsho, he left the studio following the master's death and—ever curious—investigated what other schools had to offer. In the process, he came across examples of art displaying a distinct western influence that had originally filtered through via the Dutch trading post in Nagasaki.

To appreciate the impact of such influence, it is necessary to remember that Japan underwent a policy of National Seclusion from 1639 to 1854. Foreign trade was strictly limited and the Japanese themselves forbidden to travel abroad. The pictures derived from European engravings inspired Hokusai finally to become a landscapist at the age of thirty-eight. He began work afresh, experimenting with western perspective, making endless observations; the ensuing work went into twelve volumes of the *Hokusai Manga* (sketchbooks) published in 1814.

But it was the *ukiyo-e*—"pictures of the floating world"—that made the reverse journey in the late nineteenth century to complete a circle of influences and reveal to a delighted Europe the glories of the Japanese print.

A Daimyo Musing on a Lost Love *(1835–6)*

One of a series entitled One Hundred Poems Explained by the Nurse, *this masterpiece of color printing illustrates a poem by Sanji Hitoshi. Hokusai's innate sense of proportion marries well with his development of western-style perspective; and figures of all kinds, at work and leisure, fed his insatiable enthusiasm for depicting life in all its aspects.*

Hans Holbein the Younger

Timeline

1497 Born in Augsburg, Germany, son of Hans Holbein the Elder.

1510(?)–14 Studies with father in Augsburg, then moves to Basel.

1519 Becomes member of the Basel artists' guild.

1526–28 Travels to England, with introduction to Thomas More from Erasmus. Paints portraits at the Tudor court.

1528–32 Returns to wife and two children in Basel.

1532 Abandons family in Basel. Settles in England.

1536 Attached to English Court.

1543 Dies of the plague in London.

Hans Holbein was one of two gifted sons trained by their artist father Hans Holbein the Elder. Both started out as book designers and illustrators for the leading German printer Froben of Basel, but the older boy died in 1518. In those days, printers were publishers too and their workshops were meeting places for the intellectual community. Froben's office attracted many scholars and so the young Holbein met the Dutch humanist Erasmus.

Holbein painted his first official portraits in Basel—of a burgomaster and his wife—but, despite their success, he didn't restrict himself to portraiture. He created a popular series of woodblocks called *Dance of Death*, designed stained glass, made models for goldsmiths, and painted some religious subjects. However, in 1525, as the Reformation spread throughout northern Europe, religious images came under attack in Basel and disorder even threatened the town's food supply. Artists everywhere were seeking alternative work and Holbein decided to go to England.

He sailed in 1526, having persuaded Erasmus to write a letter of introduction to Henry VIII's Treasurer, Sir Thomas More. Holbein's admission to the English Court was the key moment of his career and before long they had accepted him as their leading artist.

Together with his responsibilities for ceremonial and festive occasions at Court, Holbein provided an accompaniment to Henry's serial marriages with his portraits of the king's actual and prospective brides. But these were a mere handful among the one hundred or so, including miniatures, that he painted in total.

Sir Richard Southwell *(1536)*

When this portrait was painted, Southwell had been sheriff of Suffolk and Norfolk for two years, despite the fact that he was a convicted murderer. Holbein conveys a certain unpleasantness about the man but, as always, in his dispassionate style. The unshaven jaw below his sneering mouth draws the viewer's attention to the scars on his neck.

Anne of Cleves *(1539)*

The Tudor period was one of intrigue and deception. In this portrait of Henry VIII's fourth wife, perhaps Holbein's meticulous, blended brushstrokes smoothed over those features that caused the king to call her the "Mare of Flanders" once he had met her. Her elaborate dress certainly outshines her facial expression. Should that have been a clue? However, by the time he and Anne were wed, Henry was more or less ready to commission a portrait of wife number five.

Winslow Homer

"In the future I will live by my watercolors." Although Winslow Homer first used the medium when he was already a mature artist, he significantly raised the profile of watercolor in the United States and through several hundred works became its acknowledged master.

Homer's art training consisted of apprenticeship to a lithographer. Once he had become an illustrator for *Harper's Weekly* in New York, he seemed destined to remain so. However, a year's assignment as a Civil War artist meant expeditions to the Virginia front where he assembled a portfolio, which formed the basis for his first important oils. Unlike **Whistler** and Sargent, Homer—a reserved and unostentatious man—worked mostly in the United States and left avant-garde European movements like Impressionism to proceed without him.

His early watercolors evoked a pre-Civil-War rural idyll and stand in contrast to his war reportage. Then Homer went still further—to the north of England for two years, in fact—and produced a series based in the fishing village of Cullercoats. Steam trawlers had already begun to replace smaller fishing

Home, Sweet Home *(1863)*

As a war artist, Homer lived among the soldiers and in this picture he captures a scene with two federal infantry privates at suppertime. The band in the distance is supposedly playing "Home, Sweet Home." The men's "brogan" boots are brown, which is how they were issued. Soldiers were supposed to apply boot black to them, but often had more important duties.

craft, but Homer persisted in recording the old ways and traditional skills, as in *Mending the Nets*.

He moved to Prout Neck, Maine, after his return to New York. It became his home for the rest of his life, apart from working holidays on the New England coast, in the Adirondacks and Quebec, and the winters that he spent in warmer climes. Homer painted the sea and its people repeatedly until, finally, he omitted people in favor of the vastness of the ocean alone.

Shark Fishing *(1885)*

Homer was not the United States' first sporting artist but he did become master of the genre, just when the nineteenth-century "church" of the sublime landscape was transformed into the great outdoors and the "theater of manly enjoyment."

Edward Hopper

Timeline

The paintings of Edward Hopper are landmarks of American Realism, a style he never abandoned but did not follow merely in order to reproduce the visible. As he said, "No amount of skillful intervention can replace the essential element of imagination."

Fifty years separate *The Absinthe Drinker* from *Automat* but **Degas** stirred Hopper's awareness of what the American artist called "decaying from your original idea," with the statement: "It's much better to draw from…memory. It's a transformation in which imagination collaborates…One reproduces only…the necessary."

Although educated in the European tradition and a visitor to Paris in the early 1900s, Hopper remained unaffected by movements like Cubism, just as he avoided Abstraction later on in the United States.

"America seemed awfully crude and raw when I got back," he admitted, yet it was those qualities that rooted Hopper's disquieting vision, through which he conveys the sense of alienation that pervades any big city.

Initially trained as an illustrator, Hopper was not a good painter technically. But the severity and harsh illumination of his compositions, populated by solemn figures who at times appear scarcely more alive than the furniture, draw viewers in with a collective atmosphere. Like all significant artists, Hopper can, without a trace of sentimentality, make people look at some

The Absinthe Drinker *(1876)* by Edgar Degas
Degas' imagination accidentally transformed the reputations of two of his friends with this picture. The woman is actress Ellen Andrée, the man a painter called Desboutin. Degas portrays them sitting deep in thought, but claimed he did not mean to portray them as dissipated and degraded, which was how the critics perceived them.

commonplace image and perceive their own susceptibilies in the face of daily existence.

For over forty years, Hopper was married to Jo Nivison, his inspiration, model, and intellectual match. Jo was an artist herself, whose development was thwarted by Hopper's demands on her time. They had a studio apartment in New York and another home at Cape Cod, where Hopper represented the sunshine as the sole antidote to melancholy.

Automat *(1927)* by Edward Hopper

A woman sits alone with a cup of coffee. We can only guess if the empty chair opposite means that she's expecting someone or indeed would welcome the arrival of anyone at all. Placing her in an alienating environment where people connect only with vending machines, Hopper makes use of distance and detachment—painted and imaginary—to create a situation where the viewer supposes the consequences.

Wassily Kandinsky

Timeline

The Dream *(1911)* by Franz Marc

Marc nearly always included animals in his vivid pictures. For him, animals represented the innocence and harmony with nature that human beings had lost, and he firmly believed that art could bridge the natural and spiritual worlds. Marc died in battle at Verdun in 1916. One of his last works, Fighting Forms, *moves toward abstraction under the influence of Kandinsky. The two artists collaborated on* Der Blaue Reiter *almanac and exhibitions in 1911 and 1912. The professed desire of the group was to go "behind the veil of appearances."*

Wassily Kandinsky could hear colors. This condition—known as synesthesia—was key to his art, and he even named some of his paintings "improvisations," "lyrical," and "compositions" as though they were pieces of music. Kandinsky's pioneering development of abstract painting paralleled his need to express colors and forms as if they were plucked from the same air through which sound waves travel. He aspired to "pure painting" that would bring the viewer to the same emotional threshold as listening to a symphony: "Color is the key. The eye is the hammer. The soul is the piano with its many chords. The artist is the hand that, by touching this or that key, sets the soul vibrating automatically."

Kandinsky was thirty before he began to paint and yet became one of the most original and influential artists of the twentieth century. In 1901 he led an avant-garde movement in Munich called Phalanx. Both a school and a society, it aimed for freedom from an academy-dominated art world.

Kandinsky had a long-term relationship with one of the Phalanx students, Gabriele Münter, whose vision and experimentation influenced his style dramatically. Up to the outbreak of war in 1914, when Kandinsky had to leave Germany, Münter was present at crucial moments in his career: his first abstract painting, and the founding of the Expressionist *Der Blaue Reiter* (Blue Rider) group with Franz Marc (1880–1916). She led him to an appreciation of child art, which Kandinsky believed offered a deep spiritual understanding through which all humankind might grow.

Impression 5 *(1911)* by Wassily Kandinsky

Kandinsky's style was based on the nonrepresentational properties

of form and color, used to express the full range

of his memories, emotions, and imagination.

Leonardo da Vinci

Timeline

Leonardo da Vinci trained as an artist and craftsman but soon proved himself a scientist as well. It is not known where he learned engineering; he might even have taught himself the laws of mechanics. His notebooks reveal the scope of his originality and are full of exquisite detail. Everything is in Italian because Leonardo lacked Latin, which was probably an advantage since his work was rooted in his own observation rather than the teachings of others.

Not all Leonardo's ideas were successful. His characteristic device of *sfumato* ("in the manner of smoke") depended on slow, careful modulation of light and shade—to Leonardo strong color contrasts confused the eye. Traditional methods of fresco painting required rapid work on wet plaster, so Leonardo developed a new compound to prime the wall for *The Last Supper*. Unfortunately, it neither held the paint nor protected it from moisture.

However, what remains of the fresco demonstrates Leonardo's approach to composition. Rather than placing Christ and the apostles in a strict row, he grouped them naturally, each gesturing in reaction to Christ's statement that one of them would soon betray him. The way that the space appears to recede behind Christ's head is a classic example of one-point perspective.

Leonardo is one of the greatest painters and most versatile geniuses in history; the embodiment of the European Renaissance. His participation in a debate at court, between representatives of the arts and sciences, is reported admiringly by Vasari: "[he] silenced the learned and confounded the liveliest intellect."

La Scapigliata *(1508)*

A delicate oil study, perhaps a Madonna,

known as The Lady with Dishevelled Hair.

The Virgin and Child with St. Anne *(c. 1510)*

The stream of life flows from the head of St. Anne down

through three generations in an intricate twisting manner

known as contrapposto.

René Magritte

Timeline

Unlike most of his fellow Surrealists, René Magritte adopted an unassuming, rather dull lifestyle. The low profile was his way of ensuring that he met with as little interference as possible while concentrating on the Surrealist task of "barring from your mind all remembrance of what you have seen, and being always on the lookout for what has never been."

The tricks and puns presented in Magritte's paintings communicate on a level that contemporary viewers understand very well. We know that things are not always what they seem because we are subjected daily to thousands of media-generated images. What does the evidence of our own eyes mean anymore?

But Magritte will not let us dodge this onslaught, nor allow any situation to remain blindly accepted. He repeatedly manipulates time, scale, and viewpoint. He turns night into day. He offers mirror images that show the reverse of what we expect to see. He creates vistas through window frames juxtaposed with canvases, suggesting the possibility of finding three-dimensional reality through the flat surface of a picture; yet the viewer must see that it's all merely painted. "Everything we see hides another thing, we always want to see what is hidden by what we see."

Fantomas poster *(1925)*

The Fantomas Appreciation Society was founded by the avant-garde poet Apollinaire in 1912. René Magritte and his brother Paul shared a passion for the Fantomas films, shown in 1913 and 1914 and based on the novels by Souvestre and Allain. The fictional criminal became a source of inspiration for Magritte and often suggested his choice of titles.

The Happy Donor *(1966)*

Magritte was always conscious that things have a flip side even more curious than their façade. In order to render the "dark" side visible, several of Magritte's recurring motifs are assembled here: bowler-hatted Mr Average, the melodious cowbell (with associated cheese), and the evocative house at twilight. Being fooled allows us to "shift our gaze," as the philosopher Lacan wrote, to eventually see things for what they really are by seeing what they really aren't.

Édouard Manet

Déjeuner sur L'Herbe *(1863)*

The woman's bold stare challenges the law concerning her naked presence and that of the other woman (mixed bathing and nudity were illegal). It has been suggested that the face is that of Manet's model Victorine Meurent, but that the body belongs to Suzanne Leenhoff, mother of his half-brother and shortly to be his wife. The accompanying men are Suzanne's brother Ferdinand, a sculptor, and Manet's brother Gustave, in an "artistic" fez.

Édouard Manet was a paradoxical combination of the revolutionary artist who craved official gold medals; the debonair man-about-town who used street slang; and the republican liberal who wanted to go home to the comfortable conservative lifestyle to which he was accustomed. He was handsome, witty, and generous to friends, who included Baudelaire and Zola. And he loathed the hypocrisy of people like his own father, a pillar of the legal establishment with an illegitimate son, whose mother Manet married himself once his father was dead.

He was one of the generation regularly excluded from the Paris Salon. Rejected for both style and content, the famously controversial *Olympia* and *Déjeuner sur L'Herbe* ended up in the Salon des Refusés, although Manet really had not anticipated the power of public opinion against him. Yet, as far as his peers were concerned, *Déjeuner* marked the dawn of Impressionism. Manet's composition follows a sixteenth-century engraving of a lost drawing by Raphael, called *The Judgment of Paris*. By reinterpreting the work of a Renaissance master, Manet was questioning the possibility of belief in anything one once trusted. This painting was completed the year after the death of Manet's father, who was both a judge and an adulterer.

By 1874, Manet's reputation as experimental artist and leader of the Impressionists was firmly established. The Café Guerbois, near his Batignolles studio, became the meeting place for **Monet**, **Renoir**, Sisley (1839–99), **Degas**, and Pissarro (1830–1903) and although Manet presided over them regularly, he would not participate in their exhibitions. He chose instead to remain focused on the Salon, which he called "the true field of battle." His main influences had always been the Spanish painters **Velázquez** and Goya (1746–1828), but it was during this time— when he actually went painting *en plein air* from Monet's boat studio—that he came closest to the Impressionist style.

Lola de Valence *(1862)*

Lola de Valence was the lead dancer in a troupe from Madrid who performed at the Porte Dauphine during the summer season of 1862.

Henri Matisse

Timeline

Henri Matisse and Pablo Picasso shared artistic pre-eminence and popularity for much of the twentieth century, but there was a huge difference between them. Against Picasso's unrelenting showmanship, Matisse developed slowly and methodically, and never set out to be controversial. He once famously said he wished his art to be like a comfortable armchair to relax in at the end of a busy day. Behind the nude dancers and riot of color, Matisse was an unashamed bourgeois.

The Apparition *(1874–76)* by Gustave Moreau

Gustave Moreau, the son of a Paris architect, became leader of the Symbolists. Inspired by the fifteenth-century Italians, he was a creator of hallucinatory worlds based on myths and dreams. Matisse spoke of his teacher as an invigorating influence, although the art establishment disapproved of his methods. "He did not set us on the right roads, but off them. He disturbed our complacency." Moreau's lavish use of paint gave rise to textures that inspired Matisse's later decorative work.

Matisse took early training from Gustave Moreau (1826–98), who positively encouraged his students to question everything and to advance their own opinions. Matisse studied the works of **Manet**, Gauguin, **Van Gogh**, and **Cézanne**. Then he explored **Seurat**'s pointillism through Signac. But it was from 1904 through 1907 that he got together with Derain, Vlaminck, Braque, and other former students to experiment in the vivid colors and exaggerated style that was called Fauvism. Matisse traveled south one summer with Derain to Collioure; and that was where he first had the idea for his painting *The Dance*, while watching fishermen dancing in a circle on the beach.

After the Fauves, Matisse began to work with bolder shapes and strong patterns. Once he had moved permanently to the Côte d'Azur, his pleasure in floating bright colors onto canvas culminated in some of his most successful works.

As an old man, Matisse underwent abdominal surgery, which left him quite disabled. Undaunted, he entered yet another phase of creativity with simple colored paper cut-outs; and so, often bedridden, he carried on making art to the very end.

Still Life of Fruit and a Bronze Statue *(1910)* by Henri Matisse
Matisse allowed the colors of these objects to dictate the final composition. Warm, glowing fruits and bright ceramics leap out from the cool background, at the same time remaining integral to the arrangement. Matisse rejoiced in the use of newly invented pigments and the restoration of color's emotive power.

Michelangelo Buonarroti

Timeline

1475	Born in Caprese, Italy, son of a Florentine nobleman
1481	Death of mother
1488	Apprenticed to Ghirlandaio in Florence
1490–92	Lives in household of Lorenzo de' Medici
1496–1500	Leaves Florence. Settles in Rome, sculpts the *Pietà*
1501–04	Sculpts *David* in Florence
1505–16	Sculpts figures for tomb of Julius II
1508–12	Paints ceiling of Sistine Chapel
1534	Death of father. Leaves Florence for good. Relationships established with de' Cavalieri and Vittoria Colonna
1536–41	Paints *The Last Judgment*
1542–50	Last paintings, *Conversion of St. Paul* and *Crucifixion of St Peter*
1546	Made chief architect of St. Peter's Basilica, Rome
1547	Deaths of Vittoria Colonna and pupil del Piombo
1564	Dies of a fever in Rome

The Holy Family with Infant St. John the Baptist
(Doni tondo) (c.1506)

Painted for the birth of Agnolo Doni and Maddalena Strozzi's daughter, this is a fine example of Michelangelo's sculptural eye for intertwining bodies and the play of light on muscles and drapery. His female figures are unfailingly muscular because Michelangelo used male models, claiming that females charged more.

Michelangelo Buonarroti—like his Florentine contemporary, **Leonardo da Vinci**—is one of art's most versatile geniuses. Possibly the greatest marble sculptor in the western tradition, he was also a master painter and architect. Had he only sculpted his first *Pietà*, painted the ceiling of the Sistine Chapel, or designed St. Peter's in Rome, any one of those achievements would have ensured his place in history.

Michelangelo's ability to judge a block of marble was legendary; some even said that he could see the potential figure inside. However, for his *David*, Michelangelo was obliged to rework a forty-year-old block, previously abandoned by another sculptor.

Leading up to the commission for the Sistine Chapel ceiling, Michelangelo was in constant demand and always well rewarded. Throughout his life, he invested wisely in property for his four brothers and possessed a fortune himself at the time of his death.

His response to the Sistine Chapel assignment was to protest: "painting is not my art." The rest—as we know— is history. For four highly uncomfortable years, Michelangelo struggled to transform an odd-shaped, leaky vault with some of the most sublime and memorable images in the world.

As an old man, he devoted the final eighteen years of his life to St. Peter's Basilica. The dome that he designed was not finished in his lifetime, but he would be satisfied that it is now a world-famous architectural landmark.

Christ, the Last Judgment, Sistine Chapel *(detail) (1541)*

This fresco gave rise to controversy from the start. Christ standing, rather than sitting as the Bible states, was the chief problem. Although standing certainly seems a more authoritative position, in response to later laws against nudity another painter added spurious draperies. Level with Christ's left foot sits the martyred St. Bartholomew, holding his own flayed skin. The skin contains Michelangelo's self-portrait.

John Everett Millais

Timeline

In 1840, aged only eleven, John Everett Millais became the youngest pupil ever admitted to London's Royal Academy Schools. While there, he met Holman Hunt, who became a lifelong friend, and also Dante Gabriel Rossetti. All three agreed that the Academy had stifled British art too long with its "murky chiaroscuro." So in 1848, out of their radical discussions, the Pre-Raphaelite Brotherhood emerged to challenge orthodoxy with a colorful return to pre-Renaissance values.

The life of the Brotherhood was fairly short—six years—but spent under attack from both press and public. Millais' *Christ in The Home of His Parents* drew a venomous review from Dickens. The fuss reached the ears of Ruskin, who wrote to *The Times* in defense of the Pre-Raphaelite Brotherhood. This proved a fateful connection for Millais, who fell in love with and later married Effie, Ruskin's ex-wife. They went on to have eight children.

The passion for medievalism wore off when Millais tired of spending all day painting an area "no larger than a five shilling piece." He decided to loosen up his brushwork and settle down to being a first-class academic painter. Millais was a brilliant technician but he was no intellectual. He painted politicians and sentimental narratives without a trace of cynicism. He enjoyed the wealth and awards that his talent justly brought him; doted on his family; and kept the loyalty and affection of his friends, especially that of his fellow artists.

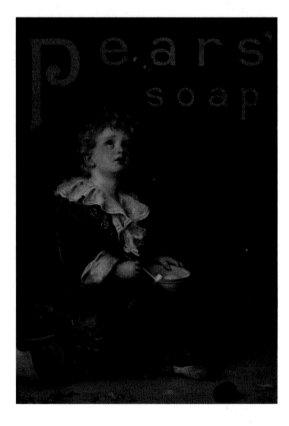

Pears' Soap Advertisement Featuring Bubbles *(1886)*

Millais' grandson, William James, was the model for this picture, originally titled A Child's World. *When bought by Pears, Millais' permission had still to be obtained for the addition of a bar of soap, for use as an advertisement.*

Bubbles remains one of the most iconic advertising symbols ever devised, and many of the color prints that Pears later published hung in homes around the world.

Ophelia *(1851–2)*

The Pre-Raphaelites experimented with every new pigment available, glazing them for maximum luminosity, onto canvas primed with zinc white. Ophelia "reads" like a color merchant's catalog, with its cobalt blue, madder lake, chrome yellow, chromium oxide, and zinc yellow. Millais began painting the background out of doors, near Kingston-upon-Thames. The painting was completed in London the following winter. Lizzie Siddal, the Pre-Raphaelite muse, wearing an antique brocade gown, had to lie in a bath of water, heated by oil lamps from below. The cold she caught as a result brought the threat of damages against the artist from Lizzie's father.

Piet Mondrian

Piet Mondrian came from a devout Calvinist family of keen painters and musicians. But their repressive discipline led to his rejection of a steady art-teaching career in favor of the artist's life itself, and later still, to his embrace of Theosophy.

This mystical belief system—in humanity's evolution toward spiritual unity—was popular in the West at the time, not least among the pioneers of abstract art, **Kandinsky** and Malevich (1879–1935). Mondrian's encounter with Cubism in 1911 was the critical point of his artistic development, when he removed natural forms from his pictorial vocabulary. Together with Theosophy, it propelled him into the ranks of the avant-garde. The obscure Dutchman left for Paris, the first step toward an international life that would have a lasting impact on western art.

Stranded in Holland by World War I, Mondrian and Theo van Doesburg (1883–1931) formed a group and published a magazine called *De Stijl* (The Style). The writer Schoenmaekers' ideas of "positive mysticism" were directly incorporated and Mondrian's aesthetic became their guiding force, committed to purifying modern art and bringing it to everyone via architecture, product design, and typography.

The very term, Neo-Plasticism, that Mondrian adopted for his geometric abstractions in 1921 was borrowed from

Interior (1919) by Theo van Doesburg

An architectural model in De Stijl style, showing marked similarities with Mondrian's principles of design.

Schoenmaekers. With his typical asymmetrical arrangements of squares and rectangles painted in primary colors divided by black bands on a white ground, Mondrian strove for transcendental experience and pure harmony.

Composition with Red, Black, Blue, and Yellow *(1928)*

by Piet Mondrian

Mondrian kept strictly to vertical and horizontal lines of composition and broke with Van Doesburg for introducing diagonals into his work in 1924. When Mondrian moved to New York, in response to his energetic new surroundings, his lines formed the all-color grids he called "boogie-woogie."

Claude Monet

Timeline

1840	Born in Paris, France, son of a ship's chandler
1858	Meets and studies with Boudin
1859	Enrols at Académie Suisse, Paris. Meets Pissarro and Courbet
1863	Paints *en plein air* with Manet and Bazille
1869	*Plein air* studies with Renoir
1870–71	Marries Camille Doncieux. Moves to London. Father dies. Returns to Argenteuil
1874	Exhibits *Impression Sunrise*
1879	Death of Camille
1883	Leases home in Giverny
1887	Exhibits in New York
1892	Marries Alice Hoschedé
1900	Paints at Giverny. Visits London, paints Thames
1908	Eyesight deteriorates
1911	Death of Alice
1915–26	Works on *Water Lilies* series
1926	Dies of lung cancer in Giverny

Claude Monet is the central figure of Impressionism. The pioneering movement had its seed in an encounter between a teenaged caricaturist and a local painter, at the shop of the only picture framer in Le Havre. There, young Monet was introduced to Eugène Boudin; Academy-trained, but one who liked to paint his beach scenes in the open air, in dabs of pure color with loose, delicate brushstrokes. That summer, Boudin taught Monet to draw and paint directly from nature, "in the light, within the atmosphere, just as things are." To honor Boudin, the Impressionists included him in their first Paris exhibition.

In April 1874, a group of artists—all Salon rejects—mounted their show in a former photographic studio. Some of the names read now like a roll of honor: **Cézanne**, **Degas**, Monet, Morisot, Pissarro, **Renoir,** and Sisley. Most critics were scathing and the term "Impressionists" was unwittingly coined by one, Louis Leroy, who reserved particular scorn for Monet's *Impression Sunrise*. Turning the joke back on Leroy, the artists adopted the name permanently.

Steam Train, La Gare Saint-Lazare *(detail) (1877)* (opposite)
One of a series of twelve railway station pictures, created at different times of the day. For his most ambitious study of the urban landscape, Monet chose Saint-Lazare, gateway to his beloved Normandy. He concentrated on the full-spectrum effects of light, smoke, and steam, building cloud shapes with curly brushstrokes. Monet was a master at adapting strokes to show how light affects texture and form.

Late Summer Haystacks
(detail) (1891)
After the Gare Saint-Lazare, Monet embarked on other series— Haystacks, Rouen Cathedral, *and* Water Lilies—*each a painstaking demonstration that atmospheric color, caused by changes in the light, can modulate a subject through the entire spectrum.*

Edvard Munch

Timeline

Edvard Munch's visits to Paris between 1889 and 1892 were vital to his development, particularly as a stimulus for German Expressionism. He studied **Van Gogh** and the Symbolists, Gauguin, Moreau, and Odilon Redon (1840–1916). The first version of *The Scream* followed in 1893. The swirling lines of color are reminiscent of Van Gogh's landscapes; the agony of the soundless scream comes directly from Munch.

"From the moment of my birth, the angels of anxiety, worry, and death stood at my side..." Death was a recurring topic for the artist; both his parents and two siblings died early. Munch survived into his eighties but suffered from chronic anxiety, psychosomatic diseases, and alcoholism. His depression once led to hospitalization. Munch's themes foreshadowed many of the preoccupations of the twentieth century: loneliness, alienation, neurosis, and sexuality. A note from his diary announces: "No longer shall I paint interiors with men reading and women knitting. I will paint living people who breathe and feel and suffer and love." He found no lasting happiness in either of his own love affairs, although he commemorated both women in *The Frieze of Life*.

Munch's art was exhibited worldwide, won awards, and attracted collectors within his lifetime. In 1937, Hitler's response was to strip his paintings from gallery walls, along with those of other "degenerate" modern masters.

Rêverie (1870) by Odilon Redon

Odilon Redon was a graphic artist and writer as well as a great Symbolist painter. Influenced by Courbet and Corot, he eventually escaped from the effects of an unhappy childhood, due to his epilepsy.

The Scream *(1893)* by Edvard Munch

"I was walking along the road with two friends," wrote Munch,
"The sun set. The sky became a bloody red. And I felt a touch of
melancholy. I stood still, leaned on the railing, dead tired.
Over the blue-black fjord and city hung blood and tongues of fire.
My friends walked on and I stayed behind, trembling with fright.
And I felt a great unending scream passing through nature."

Pablo Picasso

Timeline

1881 Born in Malaga, Spain, son of a drawing professor

1901–06 Travels between Barcelona and Paris, finally settles in Paris. "Blue" and "Rose" periods

1906–14 Paints *Les Demoiselles d'Avignon* (1906). Meets Braque; they invent Cubism and pioneer collage

1914–18 Works with Cocteau, Satie, and Diaghilev

1930s Works as sculptor, writes in surrealist style. Paints *Guernica* for 1937 Paris International Exhibition

1939–45 In France for WWII with Sabartés, Dora Maar, later Françoise Gilot

1947–49 Birth of son Claude and daughter Paloma, both by Gilot. Works as ceramicist

1954 Meets Jacqueline Roque

1961 Marries Roque. Moves to Mougins

1971 Louvre solo exhibition

1973 Dies at Mougins

"Each time I had something to say, I said it in the way I felt was right. Different motifs demand different techniques. This does not imply either evolution or progress but an accord between the idea that one desires to express and the means of expressing it." Pablo Picasso's words express what many—both critics and admirers—find so elusive and capricious about him. He never "developed" in a satisfying linear progression or stayed within a style once it had evolved. Instead, as one art historian wrote, he was like a spider "who sits watching in the center of a web…from time to time he pounces and the direction of his pounce is usually unpredictable." Picasso's ventures into ceramics, sculpture, and printmaking were all unfailingly inventive; in fact, from the painting of *Les Demoiselles d'Avignon* onward, virtually no artist could escape his influence.

Female Figure at a Table *(1912)* by Umberto Boccioni
Umberto Boccioni (1882–1916), a founder of the Futurist movement, first met Picasso through Severini in Paris, in 1911. The dialog between Milanese Futurism and Parisian Cubism was fruitful. Boccioni absorbed Picasso's technique of fusing figure and background, dissolving traditional perspective and making use of tonal modeling. Picasso's Portrait of Daniel-Henry Kahnweiler *was a major influence.*

Later on, Picasso referred to art history, creating variations on earlier masters' works through a variety of media: prints, drawings, and paintings. A prime example is the series *Las Meninas*. Picasso often turned to a specific work because he identified with it personally and, as a Spanish artist, he had always felt profound ties with **El Greco**, **Velázquez**, and Goya.

Weeping Woman *(1937)* by Pablo Picasso

The model for this intensely moving picture was surrealist photographer Dora Maar (Theodora Markovitch), Picasso's mistress and muse for seven years before a stormy separation left her broken and reclusive. Like other left-wing sympathizers in 1937, the couple's eyes were on the civil war in Spain. Maar photographed Picasso's Guernica, *the antiwar icon painted in a studio she hired in rue des Grands-Augustins, Paris.*

Piero della Francesca

Piero della Francesca appears to have led a quiet provincial life. Although Veneziano was his master, he is not recorded as belonging to any workshop, and spent most of his time in either Arezzo or Borgo Sansepolcro. He seems to have freelanced only for short periods in Rome, Ferrara, Urbino, and Florence, perhaps juggling a number of assignments at any one time.

Della Francesca's work in the field of architectural invention would have made him much sought-after, for he was also a master geometrician and the author of a learned treatise on the rules of perspective. Such expertise with scale and proportion makes his paintings visually powerful. What makes them pleasing as well is his genius for organizing color masses, carefully balanced against large pale areas to achieve unity between space and lighting.

Della Francesca worked slowly. For a fresco painter, this normally poses problems but he hung wet sheets over the plaster at night so he could return to it the next day. Oil painting on wood—such as he had probably seen in Urbino—gave him no such trouble. Della Francesca's style reflected the popularity of Flemish oil painting among the patrons of the period, which may account for the loss of esteem after his death, when tastes inevitably changed.

Battista Sforza, wife of Federico da Montefeltro *(c. 1472)*

Battista Sforza was a member of the ruling Milanese family. She bore Federico seven daughters and a son after whose birth she died. Most historians believe this portrait—one of a diptych—was painted posthumously. The background shows Urbino and the surrounding countryside.

Pala Montefeltro *(1472–74)*

The Brera altarpiece: Madonna and child with angels, saints, and Federico da Montefeltro, duke of Urbino. *The duke lost his right eye and part of his nose in a tournament and was always shown facing left. This was probably della Francesca's last work before his eyesight failed but his mastery of proportions is still remarkable. The ostrich egg hanging from the shell in the apse symbolizes the virgin birth and is echoed by the oval of the Madonna's head, placed in the precise center of the composition.*

Jackson Pollock

Timeline

Jackson Pollock's groundbreaking method helped New York to supplant Paris as the avant-garde capital of modern art. By the end of World War II, it was time for a cultural challenge from the New World. Pollock declared, "I don't see why the problems of modern painting can't be solved as well here as elsewhere," and began blazing a trail for other Abstract Expressionists. Even Willem de Kooning (1904–97) admitted, "He broke the ice." De Kooning and Pollock were friendly rivals; it was the critics who liked to champion one against the other. But de Kooning never captured the public imagination as Pollock did when he broke with tradition.

Pollock's Action painting was influenced by the Surrealists' "psychic automatism." Rejecting easel and palette, and without any preliminary sketches, he spread unprimed canvas over the floor and poured paint straight from a can, or he dripped and flicked it, using brushes and sticks. Sometimes he incorporated broken glass or wire for added texture.

Pollock is famous for the wild, drunken behavior that ultimately killed him. Yet he was a solitary individual, not one for the groups or ideologies that bonded artists in those days.

Pollock was free of the "art-historical" approach; unsophisticated and intellectually uncomplicated, his chief contribution to art was to express emotion and sensation through abstraction.

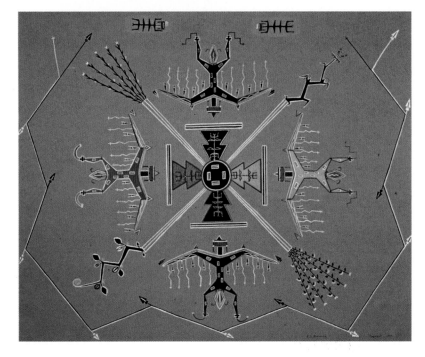

Navajo Sand Picture

Pollock developed his compositions by allowing the imagery to evolve spontaneously, without preconceptions. He called this technique "direct" painting and compared it to Native American Indian sand painting, made by trickling thin lines of colored sand onto a horizontal surface. Pollock claimed, however, that for him it was "a means of arriving at a statement."

Undulating Paths *(1947)*

His large-scale "drip paintings" are Pollock's most impressive
works, which he produced between 1947 and 1952
(Pollock abstained from alcohol from 1948 through most of
1950). Moving rhythmically, he would cover the whole canvas,
quickly interweaving pattern and color; the procedure
was always controlled and far from random.

Nicolas Poussin

Timeline

1594	Born in Les Andelys, France, son of an ex-soldier.
1612	Inspired by Varin, studies Mannerism under Lallemand in Paris.
1623	Travels to Rome via Venice.
1624	Settles permanently in Rome.
1624–30	Draws antiquities. Paints mythological scenes. Influenced by Titian and Veronese. Experiments with Baroque style.
1629	Marries Anna-Maria Dughet.
1630–40	Paints historical scenes. Influenced by Mantegna and Raphael.
1640–42	Becomes French Court painter to Louis XIII. Returns to Rome.
1642–65	Paints landscapes, continues history genre.
1665	Health declines. Dies in Rome.

Nicolas Poussin formulated the precepts of French classical and academic art, in the belief that a painting should arouse a rational and intellectual response in the viewer, not mere pleasure. His rather austere, authoritative approach to ancient history and classical mythology influenced painting as far as the nineteenth century, and most French artists from **David** to **Cézanne**.

Poussin wasn't particularly interested in the events or personalities of his time and the only portrait he ever produced was of himself. Nor was he sympathetic to the artistic factions that he found in Rome. In his opinion, the Mannerists were too affected and the Naturalists weren't refined enough. Poussin's great passion was history, and through his art he told epic, noble, and stirring tales. He undertook historical research responsibly, training himself in archeology and the study of coins, and carefully checked the authenticity of everything. He once wrote in a letter: "I am forced by my nature toward the orderly."

The Shepherds of Arcadia (detail) (1638)

In the mid-1630s, Poussin explored the work of Raphael, Roman architecture, and Latin books on moral conduct. From these he adopted the pure, classical idiom that he used for the rest of his life. The inscription "Et in Arcadia ego" is a quotation from the Latin poet Virgil. Poussin reminds us that there is no escape from death, even in the perfect world of Arcadia.

Echo and Narcissus *(1627–28)*

For a period of five years, Poussin worked on themes from classical mythology and the Renaissance poets. At the same time, he came under the painterly influence of the Venetian Titian. Pictures like this one and Rinaldo and Armida *use sensuous colors and show true feeling for their poetic sources.*

As a painter, Poussin worked prodigiously hard, and reached a highly creative and inspired phase in his mid-forties. He constructed models of wood and wax from which he made preliminary sketches, and only then did he start painting. He observed the compositional styles of Mantegna and **Raphael**, and turned to **Titian** for the study of nudes.

Pouissin's later studies of sunsets and morning in the Roman Campagna are some of his purest achievements.

Raphael Santi

Timeline

1483	Born Raffael Santi in Urbino, Italy, son of Giovanni Santi, Court painter to Federico da Montefeltro, duke of Urbino.
1491	Death of mother.
1494	Death of father.
1500	Apprenticed to Perugino in Perugia.
1504	Moves to Florence, studies Michelangelo, Leonardo, Bartolomeo, and Masaccio.
1505–07	Paints Madonnas series.
1507	Paints the *Deposition*.
1509–20	Called to Rome by Pope Julius II to paint the *Stanza*, including *School of Athens*.
1513	Death of Pope Julius II. Paints *Sistine Madonna*.
1514	Made architect of St Peter's, Rome.
1517	Paints the *Transfiguration* (unfinished).
1520	Dies in Rome.

The youngest of the three giants of the Italian High Renaissance, Raphael is best known for his Vatican frescoes, numerous Madonnas, and fascinating portraits, including the beautiful *La Fornarina* (now revealed as Raphael's secret wife) and the haunting *Pope Julius II*. Son of a Court painter, Raphael was born into the right surroundings for an artistic career and, despite being orphaned at eleven, his precocious talents ensured his survival.

Having completed his apprenticeship with Perugino, Raphael moved to Florence. There he honed his art to the Renaissance ideals of beauty and harmony, although his genius was tied by the demands of patrons.

Raphael's strength lay in his draftsmanship and, at that time, drawing was considered the foundation of all visual arts. For the last seven years of his life, he employed Marcantonio Raimondi in his Rome studio, engraving the backlog of drawings that he lacked time to convert into paintings. It was Raimondi's rendering of Raphael's *The Judgment of Paris* that suggested the pose of **Manet**'s figures in *Déjeuner Sur L'Herbe*, more than three centuries later.

When assigned to the Papal Court, Raphael was given charge of all major projects; not only paintings but architecture and the preservation of antiquities. Raphael wasn't a great innovator or discoverer, yet when he died at thirty-seven, his art showed an emotional depth that might well have matured to equal that of **Leonardo** and **Michelangelo**.

St Barbara, Sistine Madonna

(detail) (1512)

St Barbara looks out of the frame toward the imaginary congregation at the foot of the Sistine Madonna. She is as exquisite as any of his Madonnas, for whom Raphael drew on a wide range of beauties he had known. Both the coloring and composition of this painting typify Raphael's Roman period.

The Deposition of Christ *(1507)*

Raphael pays homage to Michelangelo's Doni Tondo—painted the previous year—with the kneeling woman twisting back, like Michelangelo's Virgin. His deposition group has reverently distanced itself from the scene of death on the hill and the body they carry is barely marked. The picture has all the qualities that Delacroix once listed as Raphael's most admirable: "his marvelous sobriety; his constant measure; no extravagance, no vulgarity, no triviality."

Rembrandt van Rijn

Timeline

1606	Born in Leiden, Netherlands, son of a miller.
1624	Studies in Amsterdam under Lastman.
1625	Sets up studio in Leiden, pupils include Dou.
1631	Moves to Amsterdam, becomes successful portraitist. Starts etching and first uses canvas.
1634	Marries Saskia van Uylenburgh.
1635–41	Saskia gives birth to four children; only one son, Titus, survives.
1642	Death of Saskia. Paints *The Nightwatch*.
1647	Engages Hendrickje Stoffels as housekeeper, later model and partner.
1654	Birth of daughter Cornelia by Hendrickje. Paints *Hendrickje Bathing*.
1656	Declared bankrupt. Paints *Titus Reading*.
1663	Death of Hendrickje.
1668	Death of Titus.
1669	Dies in Amsterdam.

Rembrandt van Rijn's clear empathy with the human condition makes it surprising to learn that he never traveled outside Holland. However, Lastman, his most influential teacher, had been to Italy and observed the work of **Caravaggio**. Lastman taught his pupil the technique of *chiaroscuro* (the rendering of extreme light and shade) and Rembrandt quickly learned to handle it with a skill few have ever matched.

The artist's personal life was a catalog of misfortune. His first wife, Saskia, and three of their children died very early. Rembrandt, although successful, had no head for business and disastrously expensive tastes. At his bankruptcy, an inventory of his art and antiquities showed a collection that included **Leonardo**, **Michelangelo**, **Raphael**, **Holbein**, **Titian**, and **Rubens**; and he had stores of exotic clothes, ornaments, and armor, which he used as props in his paintings.

During Rembrandt's long career, he engaged in drawing, etching, and painting. Over 2,000 of his works still exist and although he is probably best known for portraiture, particularly his own, his subjects range through biblical themes, everyday life, landscape, and nudes. In each genre he conveys a mixture of moods—he would study his own expressions in the mirror—and such depth of feeling that he endures as one of the most sympathetic and appreciated of all the great artists.

Portrait of the young Saskia *(1633)*

Saskia may never have worn this curious hat in public, since Rembrandt often painted himself and his family dressed in exotic costumes. The Dutch term 'tronie' refers to a special type of picture intended as a character study rather than a straight portrait.

Archangel Raphael Leaving the Family of Tobias *(1637)*

The Archangel Raphael helps Tobias to restore his father's sight and then flies off in a Baroque flurry of foreshortened limbs, wings, and drapery. But most impressive of all is Rembrandt's masterful use of chiaroscuro.

Pierre-Auguste Renoir

Timeline

With the arrival of the railway, the banks of the Seine beyond Paris became a popular resort for city workers. La Grenouillère at Croissy-sur-Seine was a restaurant built from several boats roped together, providing a dance floor in the evenings. This was the destination of Pierre-Auguste Renoir and Claude **Monet** one day in 1869, when the two young friends set up their easels together *en plein air* and initiated the breakthrough to Impressionism.

By 1881—the year he turned forty and began traveling round Europe and North Africa—Renoir knew it was time for a reassessment.

He decided that color was to be the servant not the master, and that he would attempt to express form more carefully by tonal relationships. Not that he altered his palette; Renoir kept to the bright colors he had always favored. In his later works, Renoir's experimentation brought an outpouring of monumental nudes and sensual young women with luminescent skin. Uncompromisingly, Renoir had always painted what pleased him and, since his days of decorating fans in the style of Watteau, Fragonard, and Boucher, his immense skill and the ability to convey charm remained entirely undiminished.

Uphill Path Through Long Grass *(1876)*

A landscape with figures, from Renoir's purest Impressionist period. Reminiscent of Monet's Wild Poppies, *it was probably painted during one of the summers that the two artists spent together at Argenteuil.*

Woman Combing Her Hair (1907–08)

Gabrielle Renard was a distant cousin who came as his son Jean's nurse, and stayed on as housekeeper and model for Renoir. When arthritis reduced his hands to claws, Gabrielle wrapped them in powdered gauze to prevent the skin adhering. Disabled as his father was, Claude Renoir recalled slipping paintbrushes between his father's fingers to enable him to paint.

Henri "Douanier" Rousseau

Timeline

An encounter with Henri "Douanier" Rousseau revealed a strange mixture of unworldly shyness and a cast-iron belief in his own artistic talent. He had undergone the usual elementary schooling but at some point he became convinced that painting was his true vocation and claimed that his parents' poverty had precluded art school.

Later, Rousseau went ahead and obtained a copyist's card for the Louvre, where he spent a lot of time studying the early Italians. He met the poets Jarry and de Gourment, who commissioned a lithograph from him for their review, *L'Imagier*, and before long Rousseau found himself admitted to the world of writers and artists. Encouraged by the company of the avant-garde—in the end he listed such names as **Picasso**, Gauguin, Delaunay, and Apollinaire among his acquaintances—Rousseau began submitting to the Salon des Indépendants, to which he remained loyal for the rest of his life.

Rousseau's paintings are termed "naïve" but this doesn't imply that they are instinctual. On the contrary, he planned his work with extreme care, using numerous sketches and picture references. Some mocked him for going as far as taking his sitters' measurements for portraits, as if he were a tailor, but he was mastering anatomy and proportion the best way he knew. Once past the preparatory stages, Rousseau's imagination took off, and the unremarkable one-time toll collector became the exotic storyteller whose unique images are now recognized and admired everywhere.

The Football Players *(detail) (1908)*
In contrast to his exotic subjects, Rousseau enjoyed featuring the everyday life of people around him, sharing their love of parties and recreation of all kinds. The striped footballers look more as if they are performing a surreal ballet.

The Snake Charmer *(1907)*

This lone musician stands like a dark Eve, calling out all the serpents from her moonlit paradise. Rousseau would often take his sketchbook to the Jardin des Plantes in Paris and—thanks to a secret arrangement with one of the gardeners—draw for hours among the jungle greenery of the hothouses. It was the nearest he would ever come to experiencing a tropical landscape.

Peter Paul Rubens

Timeline

1577	Born in Siegen, Germany, son of a lawyer.
1591–95	Apprenticed in Antwerp.
1600	Visits Venice, sees work of Titian and Veronese. Visits Florence.
1601	Visits Rome, sees work of Caravaggio.
1603	Diplomatic visit to Spain.
1605–06	Returns to Rome.
1609–14	Marries Isabella Brant, settles in Antwerp, has three children. Paints commissions for Antwerp Cathedral.
1610–20	Studio receives many Catholic commissions.
1621	Diplomatic service for Hapsburgs.
1622–25	Commissions in Paris and Antwerp.
1626	Death of Isabella.
1628–30	Negotiates peace between Madrid and London. Knighted by Charles I. Marries Helena Fourment, has five children.
1631	Knighted by Philip IV. Retires from diplomatic service.
1640	Dies of heart failure in Antwerp.

The Straw Hat (c. 1625)

A portrait of Susanna Fourment, sister of Rubens' second wife, Helena. Rubens' easel pictures were painted with a relaxed pleasure in the subjects to be found close to home.

Peter Paul Rubens was the possessor of phenomenal gifts, together with the physical energy and organizational ability to exercise them.

As well as being an exponent of the lush Baroque style that he had acquired in Italy (a key influence was **Caravaggio**, whose work Rubens continued to champion across northern Europe), he was Roman Catholic, multilingual, and appointed ambassador for the Hapsburg rulers of the Spanish Netherlands. His status as Court painter exempted Rubens from paying taxes and it also freed him from guild rules; he could deploy, without restrictions, the huge studio staff needed to carry out all his commissions, many of whom had their own specialties.

Marie de Medici Disembarking at Marseilles After Marriage
to Henry IV of France *(detail) (1622–25)*
*One of a cycle of twenty-one paintings for the Palais de Luxembourg,
commissioned by French dowager queen Marie de Medici to depict
her life. Rubens prepared hundreds of master sketches for his studio
to work from. It was no easy task diplomatically, since the queen was
quarrelsome, far from attractive, and had wasted huge amounts of
money without achieving anything remarkable in her life. To Rubens'
credit, he left a satisfied client on completion.*

These commissions chiefly consisted of dynamic imagery
designed to tempt people away from the somber Protestantism of
the Reformation. It was what the Catholic Church and European
royalty required for their propaganda purposes. Drawing upon
his Latin school education, Rubens produced scores of elaborate
altarpieces and allegorical ceilings. He was adept at painting
supposedly Christian virtue but giving it a subversive sinuosity;
the voluptuous features of his nudes are deliberately exaggerated
to emphasize fecundity and freedom from want.

Rubens' stylistic influence endured over three centuries, from
Van Dyck and Murillo, through Watteau and **Gainsborough** to
Delacroix and **Renoir**.

Georges Seurat

Georges Seurat's name is practically synonymous with the word "pointillism," a divisionist painting method that he himself called "optical painting." Seurat was a Neo-Impressionist. With Signac and, early on, Pissarro, he engaged in an analysis of the techniques used by the Impressionists to reproduce light and color.

Seurat's goal was a formula for the creation of luminous color on canvas by painting dots of contrasting colors next to one another. The effect was to be one of pure color, blended literally on the retina of the beholder and not on the painter's palette. It is reasonable to ask why an artist should seek the constraint of a formula; the answer could be lack of confidence in handling paint, or too-rigid training that rejects anything irregular or impulsive. Or, on the other hand, perhaps like other highly disciplined painters—della Francesca, **Poussin**, and Mondrian, for example—Seurat relished the intellectual challenge, loved to work "scientifically," and enjoyed the laborious process of proving his theory. Unfortunately, it didn't actually work; at least, not as predicted.

Apart from an incomplete grasp of existing color theories, Seurat and Signac didn't question the purity or relative color values of the pigments they used. The result was not the

The Sideshow *(1887–88)*

A wonderfully atmospheric, skillfully composed picture of a traveling fair, with the oil and gas lamps relieving the gloom of a winter's evening and tempting the audience to some escapist entertainment.

luminosity they had hoped for. As Signac admitted: "…red dots and green dots make an aggregate which is gray and colorless."

Of course, Seurat's works are not colorless, but nor are they rainbow bright. Instead, all those painstakingly applied dots produce the pleasant visual sensation of a light pearly haze, or grain, which has become Seurat's distinguishing mark after all.

A Sunday Afternoon on La Grande Jatte *(1884–86)*

Seurat's most famous painting, the product of many preparatory drawings and painted "rehearsals," and the centerpiece of the 8th Impressionist exhibition where it first appeared. His pointillist technique has successfully created the dreamlike suspension of time and motion on a warm, sunny afternoon beside the river.

George Stubbs

Timeline

George Stubbs had a passion for anatomy, both human and animal. He received little formal training but knew enough of the subject to teach it to medical students while in York, England; and in 1751, he illustrated Dr John Burton's *Essay Towards a Complete New System of Midwifery*. Burton was a notorious Jacobite, which could explain Stubbs' dislike of the Hanoverians and his prolonged refusal of commissions from Britain's Hanoverian king, George II.

Stubbs' exquisite anatomical drawings formed the basis of his expertise as a horse painter. For eighteen months he rented a remote Lincolnshire farmhouse where he could work undisturbed, dissecting specimens to discover the function of every bone and muscle. This led to his publication of *The Anatomy of the Horse*, which became a major reference for artists and naturalists.

In those days, horse paintings were ranked lower than landscapes. Yet, with a circle of wealthy patrons, Stubbs kept busy enough, painting top racehorses for aristocratic owners and breeders who wanted a pictorial record to accompany their stud book listings. And other commissions followed for families posing in their horse-drawn carriages.

Mares and Foals in a River Landscape *(detail) (1763–68)*
Stubbs made a series of studies of brood mares and foals set against a variety of backgrounds, from woods to mountains. His expert anatomical knowledge enabled him to pose the horses convincingly in a pleasing design. He would paint the animals first and then fill in the surrounding landscape from his imagination.

Stubbs also enjoyed painting a variety of wild animals, including lions, tigers, giraffes, monkeys, and rhinoceroses, which he observed in fashionable private menageries. He once traveled to Morocco, where he witnessed at first hand a lion stalking a horse.

Many of Stubbs' pictures were executed in thin oils and exist now in a rather fragile condition. However, most are still privately owned by the families for whom they were originally painted.

Two Foxhounds *(1792)*

A commission from the Reverend Thomas Vyner of Lincolnshire, in eastern England, who was an avid sportsman and expert breeder of foxhounds. This dog and bitch in an imaginary landscape were probably from the Earl of Yarborough's renowned Brocklesby pack.

Titian

Titian became the most celebrated painter in Venice following the premature death of Giorgione from the plague. Both were trained by the **Bellini** brothers, but Titian found them uninspiring and had joined Giorgione's studio once his apprenticeship was over. The pair were so compatible that sometimes people could not tell their work apart.

Titian evolved rapidly as a pure painter, with no "Renaissance man" distractions such as science, poetry, or architecture. *The Assumption of the Virgin*, painted for the Franciscans, attracted Alfonso d'Este, duke of Ferrara, who ordered three mythological studies from Titian's workshop for his personal gallery. The duke's *studiolo* had alabaster walls and a gold ceiling. It was a commission marred only by Este himself, whose manner alternated between flattery and bullying.

Later in his career, when his work had matured throughout the demands and adulation of so many kings, princes, and popes, Titian came to value the exploration of color above any other aspects of art. All his life he had known how to extract the best from his materials and he advanced to a tonal painting style, using not only brushstrokes but also his fingers and pieces of rag (he claimed he did this to avoid looking like **Raphael**). *The Death of Actaeon* and *Tarquin and Lucretia* are two outstanding confirmations of Titian's later supremacy, which point forward to the heirs of his influence, among them most notably **Delacroix**, Goya, **Rembrandt**, **Renoir**, **Rubens**, **Van Dyck**, and **Velázquez**.

Pope Paul III, Alexander Farnese *(1543)*

Alexander Farnese, the last of the Renaissance popes and a veteran politician, was seventy-five at the time Titian painted this portrait. A patron of the arts and a reformer who later summoned the Council of Trent, Farnese was the pope responsible for excommunicating Henry VIII of England from the Roman Catholic church.

Bacchus and Ariadne *(1522)*

One of three mythological subjects painted for the Duke of Ferrara's studiolo between 1518 and 1525. For this picture, Titian first painted the background in full. Each foreground figure was then filled in over a silhouette of white ground, for the richest color effect. His palette included most of the pigments known to the workshops of the day. The composition of the painting is complex but so skillfully accomplished that every detail of the story unfolds smoothly as the eye travels round.

Joseph Mallord William Turner

Timeline

1775	Born in London, England, son of a barber.
1785	Lives with uncle in Brentford on Thames.
1790	Enters Royal Academy Schools.
1791–94	Lives in Bristol, sketching tours in Britain.
1796	First oil shown at Academy, *Fishermen at Sea*, influenced by Wilson and Poussin.
1798–1818(?)	Lives with mistress. Sarah Danby; they have two daughters.
1802	Member of Academy. First visit to Europe (Paris and Alps), influenced by Claude Lorrain.
1804	Death of mother. Opens London gallery.
1805–25	Lives near Thames at Isleworth and Twickenham.
1819	First visit to Italy.
1829	Death of father. Suffers depression.
1838	Paints *The Fighting Temeraire*.
1844	Paints *Rain, Steam and Speed*.
1851	Dies in London.

The name of J.M.W. Turner is closely associated with London's Royal Academy. He became a full member when only twenty-seven, never missed showing at the annual exhibition, and served as a member both of the Council and the hanging committee. He even lectured in landscape painting for seventeen years. Altogether, Turner sounds like a thoroughly respectable Academician who could be relied upon to produce the sort of "brown gravy" paintings that the Impressionists rejected half a century later.

However, Turner's fellow Academicians on Varnishing Days could tell a very different story. Varnishing Days allowed exhibitors to retouch their work before the varnish went on. Turner would arrive, complete with top hat, to attend to several pallid canvases that looked "like chaos before the creation," and set to work "with all the brightest pigments he could lay his hands on...until they literally blazed with color." Many Academicians looked askance at Turner's apparent lack of social grace, but to hang next to him and risk being eclipsed by his works was a fate they all dreaded. Even Constable, no stranger to criticism of his own bright "nasty green," was heard to exclaim, "He's just been here and fired a gun."

Crossing the Brook *(1815)*

This Devonshire scene has been given the "Claude" treatment so expertly that rural England could easily be mistaken for Italy. Turner had learned to draw and color topographical views in the mid-1790s when he and Girtin were employed together by Thomas Monro.

Fire at Sea *(1835)*

Turner adored the sea and painted it in all its moods. The ship at the center of this catastrophe is the Indiaman Orontes. It was not the sea that destroyed her but a bundle of straw set alight by a candle in the purser's store. Turner whirls the smoke and flames into one huge vortex with the sea and sky. The mass of white and gold in the foreground contains crowds of figures that look like some kind of heavenly host, until the viewer realizes with a jolt that these are the luckless passengers, losing their struggle against the two major elements of fire and water.

Turner had indeed fired a gun—or at any rate a starting pistol—for the run up to Impressionism. Around fifty years later, in Rouen, **Monet** set up his easel at the second-floor window of a shop opposite the cathedral. He had decided to follow the example of Turner, whose gouache sketch of Rouen Cathedral he had once seen in London and never forgotten.

Anthony van Dyck

Timeline

1599	Born Antonio van Dijck in Antwerp, Belgium, son of a silk merchant.
1609	Apprenticed to Hendrik van Balen in Antwerp.
1613	Paints first portrait.
1618	Master of Antwerp Guild of Painters.
1620	Reported to have joined studio of Rubens.
1620–21	First visit to England.
1621	Returns to Antwerp.
1621–27	Works on commissions in Italy.
1627–32	Returns to work in Antwerp. Paints portraits and religious subjects.
1632–34	Works in London. Appointed Court painter to Charles I.
1634	Returns to Antwerp.
1635	Returns to settle in London.
1639	Marries Mary Ruthven; they have one daughter.
1640–41	Travels between London, Antwerp, and Paris.
1641	Dies in London.

In 1632, Anthony van Dyck became Court painter to Britain's King Charles I, who presented the celebrated Flemish artist with an allowance and a riverside house in Blackfriars, London. Van Dyck remained in the English capital for most of the rest of his life.

He and the king understood each other perfectly. Charles wanted an image that was not just a likeness but symbolic of his right to rule, while Van Dyck—familiar with the nobles of Antwerp and Genoa—was ambitious for wealth and status. Just three months after his arrival in London, he received a knighthood and a valuable chain and medal. He later portrayed himself holding the gold chain and pointing jubilantly to an enormous sunflower.

Van Dyck painted dozens of portraits of Charles, Henrietta Maria, and the royal children—with and without their dogs and horses. His success was confirmed by increased orders from the aristocracy. Having worked with **Rubens**, Van Dyck knew about busy studios. He organized his own to keep apace with one portrait per week, painting the faces of the sitters himself, before instructing his helpers to paint the garments, which they modeled on dummy figures. Van Dyck then added the finishing touches.

What emerged was a spectacular body of work that chronicles the elegant Cavalier style and profoundly influenced portraiture for over a century. Lely and Kneller owe much to Van Dyck; and his most ardent eighteenth-century follower was **Gainsborough**.

Henrietta of France, Queen of England

(1632–38)

Van Dyck had an eye for the texture of fine fabrics from a very early age. The queen's serene appearance in her magnificent yellow gown makes it difficult to believe misfortunes lay ahead of her — war and the execution of her husband.

Lords John and Bernard Stuart *(1638)*

Van Dyck was expert at composing the double portrait. The resplendent Stuart brothers present three-quarter views to the onlooker, at the same time facing each other as if they were about to dance. The empty glove held by Lord Bernard is a common device to make the fingers of his left hand look longer. Pictured here shortly before a three-year tour of Europe, both brothers ultimately died for the royalist cause in the Civil War.

Jan van Eyck

Timeline

The foremost Flemish painter of the fifteenth century led a double life for the first half of his career. Jan van Eyck's appointment as Court painter and valet to Philip the Good of Burgundy was a useful cover for secret diplomatic missions to Spain and Portugal. However, after his move to Bruges, where they welcomed him as both an artist and a city councillor, he produced several signed and dated works without interruption. His patrons included Chancellor Rolin and Canon van der Paele, for whom Van Eyck painted two outstanding Madonnas.

Van Eyck and his brother Hubert—whose death left Jan to complete the Ghent Cathedral altarpiece—are usually credited with the invention of oil painting. The truth is rather more complex and comes from Van Eyck's desire to perfect a pigmented oil already employed to tint decorative metals.

Most importantly, Van Eyck realized that painters should use properly refined drying oils like poppy or linseed. Glazing layers gave stable colors, deeper than tempera, but this many-layered oil method needed patience. Tempera had the advantage of being quick-drying. Van Eyck's genius combined the two, applying layers of oil color over a tempera ground. This yielded a full range of saturated hues; also new mixtures, because now the particles were coated in oil, adverse reactions between ingredients were avoided. Such care over the constituents ensured that Van Eyck's colors remain as fresh as the day he set down his brush.

The Arnolfini Portrait *(1434)* (opposite)

This is probably not a marriage portrait; civil registers in Lille date Giovanni Arnolfini's marriage as 1447, thirteen years later. So who is the woman in green? One theory points to Arnolfini's somber clothes and suggests it is a tribute to an earlier relationship that ended with her death in childbirth. St Margaret, the patron saint of childbearing, is carved upon the bedpost, and a single votive candle burns in the candelabra for the repose of the mother's soul.

The Madonna with Canon Joris van der Paele *(detail) (1436)*

The inclusion of the Canon's spectacles is significant. Being wealthy and well-connected, Van Eyck almost certainly had access to optical aids—mirrors and lenses—to assist his image-making.

Vincent van Gogh

Timeline

1853 Born in Groot-Zundert, Netherlands, son of a Dutch Reform pastor.

1869 Junior clerk at Goupil & Cie in The Hague.

1873–76 Works for Goupil in London and Paris.

1876 Teaches in England.

1877–79 Studies theology and preaches in Belgium.

1879–80 Studies art in Brussels.

1881–83 Sets up studio in The Hague, adopts model Sien Hoornik and family.

1883–85 Returns to parents in Nuenen. Death of father.

1886–88 Lives in Paris with brother Theo, meets contemporary artists.

1888 Moves to Arles. Gauguin visits him, severed ear incident follows quarrel.

1889–90 Voluntary patient in Saint-Rémy asylum.

1890 Moves to Auvers-sur-Oise. Produces 76 pictures. Shoots himself, dies two days later.

Sunflowers, starry nights, a severed ear, and suicide: a compelling mixture to anyone looking for an example of tragic genius. And if Vincent van Gogh's passions and difficulties are not clear enough from his canvases, we may also read the letters he wrote to his art dealer brother, Theo.

Van Gogh's first job was as an art dealer's assistant in The Hague. He taught himself to draw earlier but didn't paint until his late twenties, after failing every attempt to become a preacher, thanks to the erratic behavior that blighted all his relationships.

For two years "the Dutchman" lived in Paris with Theo, who was helpful in introducing him to many artists, including the Impressionists. Their combined influence transformed Van Gogh's previously somber palette to something "very much alive, very strong in color…"

Painting at a fantastic rate, Van Gogh achieved his greatest works during the last two years of his life. From the blissful summer warmth of Provence in 1888, he declared: "I am not conscious of myself any more…the picture comes to me as in a dream…"

The Chair and the Pipe *(1888–89)*

Van Gogh's own "white deal chair," painted as a pendant (companion piece) to Gauguin's armchair. Both chairs were symbolic portraits of the two men, painted in a rare period of calm, shortly after Gauguin's arrival at the Yellow House in Arles.

But a violent outburst following Gauguin's arrival in Arles led to a year's stay for Van Gogh in Saint-Rémy asylum. Later, Theo moved his brother north again, to Dr Gachet's care in Auvers-sur-Oise. Van Gogh died there in July 1890, from a self-inflicted gun wound. Together with masses of yellow flowers around his deathbed in a tiny room at the inn, Theo lovingly arranged no fewer than seventy-six paintings. Van Gogh's creative energy had produced them all within his final seventy days.

Starry Night Over the Rhone (1889)

Van Gogh's desire to paint a starry night sky was something he mentioned repeatedly in his letters throughout 1888. The result was this study of Arles, as he described it to Eugène Boch: "The town lighted with gas reflected in a blue river. Over it the starry sky with the Great Bear—a sparkling of pink and green on the cobalt blue field of the night sky, whereas the lights of the town and its ruthless reflections are red gold and bronzed green."

Diego de Silva y Velázquez

Timeline

Diego de Silva y Velázquez went to Madrid seeking royal patronage and, with the help of the king's minister, Count Olivares, managed to secure a place at the Spanish Court before his twenty-fifth birthday. Court painters, however talented, had to be aware of complex rituals. Velázquez "…sailed into the current that had been running deep through royal portraiture…the public image of the Spanish Hapsburgs [had become] codified through the interpretations of Titian and Antonis Mor."

It was an advantage that Velázquez and Philip IV were both young. Their developing friendship meant that the artist was not overawed by Madrid etiquette and, fortunately, his portrayal of the king won acceptance straightaway. Velázquez' career went from strength to strength, using the "keen eye and prodigious facility with the brush" that his teacher and biographer Pacheo noted from his earliest days.

But he possessed more than a polished technique; **Rubens** praised his "modestia," a kind of quiet authority. Velázquez had a gift for identifying, and communicating, truth of character through his works, as well as the obvious ability to record a likeness. He was as interested in the human condition of a band of Court dwarfs as he was in disclosing the ruthless edge of Pope Innocent X.

Margarita Teresa in a Blue Dress *(detail) (1659)*

The Infanta Margarita—the charming central figure from Las Meninas *(1656)—here seems remote and imprisoned by her formal court dress. Velázquez was instructed to paint regular portraits of the princess, which were sent to the Austrian court to record her progress. She had been betrothed as a baby to Prince Leopold.*

The twentieth-century artist Francis Bacon famously worked on his own interpretation of Velázquez' *Pope Innocent X*: "I became obsessed…it haunts me, and opens up all sorts of feelings and areas of…imagination in me."

Old Woman Cooking Eggs *(1618)*

This type of picture is known as a bodegón, *literally Spanish for "tavern" but generally meaning still life based on a kitchen scene. All the objects are strongly lit from the front and demonstrate a variety of surfaces and textures. It is thought that Velázquez painted this as an advertisement for his skills, and took it with him when he went to Madrid looking for patronage.*

115

Johannes Vermeer

Timeline

1632	Born in Delft, Netherlands, son of a silk weaver/art dealer.
1644(?)	No records in Delft, trains in Utrecht or Antwerp.
1650s	Paints historical and religious subjects.
1652	Death of father, inherits family inn.
1653	Member of St Luke's Guild. Marries Catharina Bolnes, they go on to have eleven children.
1654	Birth of first daughter, Maria.
1660s	Changes to painting genre subjects, influenced by Dou and Van Mieris.
1663	Birth of first son, Johannes.
1670s	Business suffers on French invasion of Netherlands.
1675	Physical and mental health deteriorates. Dies in Delft.

The Dutch school of the seventeenth century produced, in effect, a documentary of every aspect of their daily lives. Each painter had his specialty, from tall ships to dead pheasants. Johannes Vermeer was chiefly concerned with interiors and with one room in particular. It features in so many of his carefully composed works, lit from the left by two windows, it has a tiled floor and one map-hung wall. People within this space always seem intent upon what they are doing but in a very detached way.

Vermeer's painted tranquil images did not tally with his real-life situation; he and his wife had eleven children. However, there is evidence that Vermeer built himself a space into which, in a sense, he could retreat—a *camera obscura*. It stood at one end of that familiar room, and Vermeer arranged his subjects at the other.

First advocated for artists in the 1550s, the *camera obscura* can be made to any size. A simple darkened box, it has a pinhole or—in Vermeer's case—a lens in the side. The image of an object outside passes through the aperture and appears upside down on a blank canvas fixed to the interior wall. Vermeer would oil-sketch the projected image in black and white; X-ray analysis reveals it beneath the color layers. Then he would emerge from his "camera" to paint slowly and meticulously the finished version in full daylight.

Girl With a Pearl Earring *(c. 1665)*
The unknown girl is dressed oriental-style in a turban, which means that the picture is probably a tronie, or character study. In its fresh simplicity and directness, it is one of Vermeer's most popular images.

The Astronomer *(1668)*

This painting reminds us that Vermeer lived in an age of scientific discovery. He grew up in Delft with the inventor of the microscope, Van Leeuwenhoek, who after Vermeer's death became trustee for his estate. The astronomer's globe was made by Hondius in 1600. It sits on a table draped with an exotic cloth and the astronomer wears a flowing gown, as if the scholarly scientific future has still to contend with the superstitious past.

Paolo Veronese

Timeline

Together with Titian and Tintoretto, Paolo Veronese dominated the Venetian art scene during the sixteenth century. Although a native of Verona, Veronese of the Most Serene Republic might have been a fitting title for him. His works exhibit all the opulence that Venice had gathered through centuries of commerce and conquest. He thought nothing of painting religious scenes in a Venetian setting with the saints in silks and jewels, and although some reproached him for it, others admired this flattering portrayal of their city state.

In 1563, Veronese completed the *Marriage at Cana,* signaling a talent for architectural set pieces. Soon, more orders were placed for banquet pictures and in 1572, the Dominican convent of SS. Giovanni e Paolo requested a replacement *Last Supper* for the Titian they had lost in a fire. Veronese produced a magnificent work of arches, pillars, and staircases, bustling with fashionable people, servants, and dogs. In the middle, dwarfed by their surroundings, sit Jesus and the apostles.

Pharaoh's Daughter: The Finding of Moses (detail) (1570–75)

The Egyptian princess and her entourage, complete with dwarf jester, have come straight from a gathering at a Venetian palazzo; with calm assurance, Veronese transports the Bible story and the viewer to his own special world. As he told the Inquisition tribunal: "Painters take the same liberties as poets and jesters."

Before long, Veronese found himself before the Holy Office of the Inquisition, who objected to his *Last Supper* because it included irreverent elements not mentioned in the Bible, like a jester with a parrot and drunken German soldiers. Veronese stoutly defended an artist's right to use his imagination to fill up the space on his canvas and a compromise was reached by altering the title to *Feast in the House of Levi*, which the Bible says was attended by "publicans and sinners." Veronese was thankfully released to return to his palette.

The Marriage at Cana *(detail) (1562–63)*

The occasion of Jesus' first miracle, changing water to wine, takes place against a monumental backdrop of classical colonnades. The main players in this set-piece drama would have been readily recognizable, since Veronese included portraits of Francis I of France, Mary I of England, and Charles V of Spain. The musicians are none other than Titian, Veronese himself playing the viola, his brother Benedetto, Tintoretto, Jacopo Bassano, and Palladio.

Andy Warhol

Timeline

1928	Born Andrew Warhola in Forest City, PA, son of a miner.
1942	Death of father.
1945–49	Studies at Carnegie Institute of Technology, Pittsburgh.
1949	Commercial artist with *Vogue* and *Harper's Bazaar*.
1956	Goes on world trip.
1960	Paints first Coca-Cola bottles.
1962	Paints first Campbell's soup tins. First rents Factory attic.
1963	Makes first film, *Sleep*.
1965–68	Meets and collaborates with Velvet Underground. Factory moves site.
1968	Shot and severely injured by Valerie Solanas.
1975	Publishes *Philosophy of Andy Warhol*.
1980	Works on video tape and private cable TV.
1986	Makes last print series.
1987	Dies following routine surgery in New York.

Pop artist Andy Warhol's early days as a commercial artist primed him for the world of advertising imagery and clichéd celebrity that he so coolly invaded in the 1960s. By the end of that decade he had marked out a new arena of activity, the essential element being that he should be the one to decide what happened there. At his New York studio, called The Factory, he and his assistants quite literally reproduced the American state of mind. They flattened it onto a mesh, squeezed ink through it, and hung it out to dry—over and over again. Unique artwork was a thing of the past.

The Factory was more than a workplace, it became a fashionable drop-in center for artists and musicians and home to the "Warhol superstars"—including the rock band Velvet Underground—who formed his social set and featured in his films. Warhol's film-making totaled over sixty productions. His debut, *Sleep*, lasted six hours but actually repeated a single twenty-minute sequence—like the screenprinted dollar bills—until the mind switched from looking intently to passive acceptance.

Warhol's near-fatal shooting by Valerie Solanas, one of the Factory workers, left him in chronic pain from 1968 onward. He did produce more silkscreens and videos, but his strategy had already worked, thereby demonstrating that second- and third-hand experiences are too often accepted for real ones. More than any other twentieth-century figure, he permanently altered the concept of art.

Crime Scene of David "The Beetle" Beadle *(1939)*

A scene-of-crime shot by "Weegee," the photographer who inspired Warhol's silk-screen prints of violent news stories, such as riots and car crashes. Warhol openly incorporated the photographic image into his artwork at a time when people were not sure whether photography and art could be mentioned in the same breath.

Mao 1973 (1973)

Warhol returned to hand-painting in combination with silk-screen to produce the Mao Zedong series. The Chinese Communist leader and his "Words"—known and sold everywhere as the Little Red Book—had a cult following among young westerners. Mao's unlikely acceptance into a capitalist society was enough for Warhol to include him in his gallery of famous heads.

James Abbott McNeill Whistler

Timeline

1834	Born in Lowell, MA, son of a railway engineer.
1855	Moves to Paris. Studies under Gleyre. Begins etching.
1859–92	Settles in London. Produces Thames etchings.
1861	Paints mistress, Joanna Hiffernan, as *The Little White Girl*.
1866	Trip to South America.
1872	Begins Thames *Nocturnes*.
1876	Decorates Peacock Room for Leyland, quarrels, loses patronage.
1877	Exhibits *Falling Rocket*.
1878	Sues Ruskin for libel and wins.
1879–80	Bankrupt. Moves to Venice.
1884–86	One-man shows in London.
1888	Marries Beatrice "Trixie" Godwin.
1891	Sells to French and Scottish collections.
1892	Moves to Paris.
1896	Beatrice dies.
1903	Dies in London.

Arriving in Paris from the United States in 1855, James Abbott McNeill Whistler was surrounded by a sea of artistic talents, which included Courbet, **Degas**, Fantin-Latour, **Manet**, and Pissarro. He studied under Gleyre, with English students who relished his flamboyance and sharp wit. Yet, behind the dandified exterior was a serious spirit who only wanted to make art.

Whistler moved to London and showed his first significant work, *The Little White Girl (Symphony in White, No. 1)*, at the Academy. Speculation abounded. Was she in a trance? A nervous young bride? To everyone Whistler gave his longstanding reply: "There is no story." But an exercise in shades of white was incomprehensible to the Victorians, and so was "his abhorrence of narrative, his refusal to moralize through art, his preference for the exquisitely designed moment over the slice of life: these were new."

Despite French studio training, Whistler's truest inspiration was the Japanese print. It informed his later paintings, including the *Nocturne* that provoked Ruskin's libelous comment about the "pot of paint thrown in the public face." Whistler's *Times* obituary recounted wryly: "The trial was painful to many, amusing to more; in the end Mr Whistler obtained one farthing damages." But it also affirmed: "He was set upon…painting and etching what he saw, with no ulterior thought of utility, or popularity, or what would advance him in position and esteem. 'Art for Art'… the doctrine that Whistler professed and practised to the end."

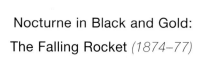

Nocturne in Black and Gold:
The Falling Rocket *(1874–77)*

Whistler's Thames Nocturnes, *painted in the 1870s, were inspired by Japanese prints. This* Nocturne, *with its spangled sky, gave rise to the Whistler's famous dispute with critic John Ruskin.*

Arrangement in Grey and Black No. 1: The Artist's Mother *(1871)*

Whistler's enterprising, puritan mother arrived uninvited from the United States to live with her "own dear butterfly" in his London home, and posed for him one day when he had no model. Standing was hard for her, so he seated his mother in profile—and an icon was born. With Japanese echoes, Whistler painted her as an austere arrangement of tones. He used black as the basis of his palette and much turpentine, which sank into the unprepared canvas to give a dulling effect that pleased him. It is Whistler's "no narrative, no sentiment" approach that has ensured her timeless appeal.

123

Glossary

Abstraction The practice of dealing with generalized concepts rather than specific, real, or literal events.

allegory A story or image that uses symbolism to put across a moral, political, or spiritual message.

avant-garde Related to art that features innovative and experimental ideas and methods.

chiaroscuro The use of contrasting light and shade in a painting or drawing.

Cubism A highly influential early 20th century movement in the visual arts. Key concepts in cubism are the rejection of a single perspective, the analysis of objects into their constituent parts, and the reconstruction of objects in abstract, geometric forms.

draperies Fabric or clothing hanging in loose folds.

en plein air This French term, meaning "in the open air," is often used to describe the practice of outdoor painting.

Expressionism An early 20th century artistic movement that attempted to represent the subjective world of emotions and personal experience, rather than objective reality.

Fauvism An artistic movement of the 1900s, the name of which was derived from the French word "fauve," meaning wild beast. Fauvism was characterized by the use of vivid, non-naturalistic colors, and had an important influence on later the Expressionists.

Futurism An artistic movement of the early 20th century, originating in Italy, which rejected traditional artistic values in favor of a new aesthetic that embraced and celebrated concepts associated with the future, such as technology, dynamic movement, and motorized transportation.

gouache A type of paint in which watercolor pigments are bound together with a gluelike binding agent, or the artistic technique using such paint.

humanism A philosophical outlook that elevates human concerns and ideas, rather than spiritual matters or beliefs, to a position of prime importance. Humanists endeavor to understand the world and find solutions to its problems by purely rational means.

Impressionism An art movement, originating in France in the 1860s, that was characterized by a desire to objectively capture the experience of a moment in time, and that placed a special emphasis on the naturalistic and accurate depiction of light.

Jacobin Related to a political club formed in the wake of the French revolution, which although initially moderate, later became infamous for the extremism and violence of its views.

Mannerism A European artistic movement, originating in Italy in around 1520, which was characterized by the use of exaggerated human proportions, unusual perspectives, and bright colors.

Metafisica Also known as Metaphysical Painting, this movement in Italian art (between 1911 and 1920) depicted fictitious and disturbing spaces, such as strange piazzas and claustrophic interiors, populated by expressionless statues and mannequins, and other objects such as balls and instruments.

mordant A substance that fixes a dye to a material such as a fabric.

124

patron An individual who financially supports a person, such as an artist, or an institution, such as an arts organization or charity.

pietà A representation of the Virgin Mary holding the dead body of Jesus Christ, in the wake of his crucifixion.

Realism The attempt to accurately and objectively depict of an artistic subject. Realism is sometimes used in the more specific sense of an artistic movement, originating in France in the 1850s, which rejected the emotionality of the Romantic movement in favor of a more honest and objective representation of reality.

Renaissance A cultural movement, originating in Italy, that transformed European art, politics, education, literature, and science between 14th to the 16th centuries. During the Renaissance, European art was revolutionized by the use of realistic linear perspective, and the systematic study of light and anatomy.

Romantic movement An artistic movement of the late 18th and early 19th century that rejected the rationalism and restraint of the Renaissance and drew inspiration from passionate and subjective feeling.

sepia A dark, reddish-brown color associated with early photographs.

Surrealism An artistic movement originating in the 1920s, which was characterized by the juxtaposition of incongruous objects and the depiction of images drawn from dreams and the subconscious.

tempera A painting technique widely used in Europe between the 12th and 15th centuries, in which powdered pigments were mixed with egg yolk and water.

triptych A piece of art featuring three decorated panels.

For Further Reading

Buchholz, Elke Linda, Susanne Kaeppele, Karoline Hille, Irina Stotland, and Gerhard Buhler. *Art: A World History*. New York, NY: Abrams Books, 2008.

Editors of Phaidon. *The 20th Century Art Book*. New York, NY: Phaidon Press, 2007.

Mancoff, Debra N. *50 American Artists You Should Know*. New York, NY: Prestel, 2011.

Strickland, Carol. *The Annotated Mona Lisa: A Crash Course in Art History from Prehistoric to Post-Modern*. Kansas City, MO: Andrews McMeel Publishing, 2007.

Web Sites

Due to the changing nature of Internet links, Rosen Publishing has developed an online list of Web sites related to the subject of this book. This site is updated regularly. Please use this link to access the list:

http://www.rosenlinks.com/gph/artis

Index

Acknowledgments

Images reproduced with permission from the following:

Art Archive (Picture Desk): 6, 7, 8, 9, 10, 12, 13, 14, 15, 16, 17, 18, 19, 21, 22, 23, 24, 25, 26, 27, 29, 30, 31, 32, 33, 34, 35, 36, 38, 40, 42, 43, 44, 45, 46, 47, 48, 49, 51, 52, 53, 55, 58, 60, 62, 63, 64, 65, 67, 68, 69, 70, 72, 75, 76, 78, 79, 80, 83, 84, 85, 86, 87, 88, 89, 90, 91, 92, 93, 94, 95, 97, 98, 99, 100, 101, 102, 103, 104, 105, 106, 107, 111, 112, 113, 117, 118, 119, 121

AKG Art Library: 37

Bridgeman Art Library: 71, 73, 77, 122

Corbis: 11, 20, 28, 39, 41, 50, 54, 56, 57, 59, 66, 74, 81, 82, 96, 108, 109, 110, 114, 115, 116, 120, 123

Salvador Dali
p 29 © Salvador Dali, Gala-Salvador Dali Foundation, DACS, London 2005

David Hockney
p 51: *Mr and Mrs Clark and Percy* 1970–71. Acrylic on canvas. 84 x 120 inches
© David Hockney

Edward Hopper
p 61: *Automat* Des Moines Art Center Permanent Collections; Purchased with funds from the Edmundson Art Foundation, Inc., 1958.2

Wassily Kandinsky
p 63 © ADAGP, Paris and DACS, London 2005

René Magritte
p 67 © ADAGP, Paris and DACS, London 2005

Henri Matisse
p 71 © Succession H Matisse/DACS 2005

Piet Mondrian
p 77: *Composition with Red, Black, Blue and Yellow* 1928
Oil on canvas, 18 x 18 inches. © 2005 Mondrian/Holtzman Trust, c/o HCR International, Warrenton, Virginia

Edvard Munch
p 81: *The Scream* 1893. Tempera on board. 33 x 26 inches. Munch Museum, Oslo.
Artwork: © Munch Museum/Munch Ellingsen Group, BONO, Oslo/DACS, London 2005
Photo: © Munch Museum (Andersen/de Jong)

Pablo Picasso
p 83 © Succession Picasso / DACS 2005

Jackson Pollock
p 87 © ARS, NY and DACS, London 2005

Andy Warhol
p 121 © The Andy Warhol Foundation for the Visual Arts, Inc./ARS, NY and DACS, London 2005